MASS STIPENDS

A DISSERTATION

SUBMITTED TO

THE FACULTY OF CANON LAW

OF THE

CATHOLIC UNIVERSITY OF AMERICA

IN PARTIAL FULFILLMENT OF THE REQUIREMENTS FOR THE DEGREE OF

DOCTOR OF CANON LAW

BY

THE REVEREND
CHARLES FREDERICK KELLER, S. T. B., J. C. L.
OF THE ARCHDIOCESE OF PHILADELPHIA

WASHINGTON, D. C.
1925

NIHIL OBSTAT:
+THOMAS JOSEPH SHAHAN, S. T. D.,
Censor Deputatus.

IMPRIMATUR:
+M. J. CURLEY, D. D.,
Archiepiscopus Baltimorensis.

SACRA FACULTAS CANONICA

UNIVERSITAS CATHOLICA AMERICAE
WASHINGTONII

1924-1925

No. 27.

CONTENTS

BIBLIOGRAPHY

SOURCES

ACTA APOSTOLICAE SEDIS. Romae, 1909.

BULLARII ROMANI CONTINUATIO. Prati, 1844.

CANONES ET DECRETA CONCILII TRIDENTINI. Romae, 1905.

COLLECTANEA S. CONGREGATIONIS DE PROPAGANDA FIDE. Romae, 1907.

CODEX IURIS CANONICI. Romae, 1918.

CODICIS I. C. FONTES. Romae, 1923 and 1924.

CORPUS IURIS CANONICI. Lipsiae, 1922-1923.

CORPUS IURIS CIVILIS. Torino, 1911.

CONCILIA PROVINCIALIA. Baltimorensi, 1842.

REFERENCES

ALEXANDER, NATALIS, *Theologia Dogmatica et Moralis.* Venetiis, 1705.

ALPHONSUS LIGUORI, *Theologia Moralis.* Tornaci, 1898.

ALZOG, *Universalgeschichte der Christlichen Kirche.* Mainz, 1855.

AMERICAN ECCLESIASTICAL REVIEW. Philadelphia, 1908.

AQUINAS, THOMAS, *Summa Theologica.* Romae, 1894.

AUGUSTINE, CHARLES, *A Commentary on Canon Law.* St. Louis, 1920.

ARCHIV FÜR KATHOLISCHES KIRCHENRECHT. Mainz, 1892.

ARENDT, *De Laesione Iustitiae Commutativae in Missae Manualis Stipendio Alteri Celebranti Diminuto.* Prati, 1914.

BALLERINI-PALMIERI, *Opus Theologicum Morale.* Prati, 1893.

BARGILLIAT, *Les Honoraires de Messes.* Parisiis, 1905.

BENEDICT XIV, *Tractatus De Missae Sacrificio.* Mechlin, 1860.

BENEDICT XIV, *Idem apud Opera Omnia.* Prati, 1843.

BENEDICT XIV, *Institutiones Ecclesiasticae.* Romae, 1784.

BENEDICT XIV, *De Synodo Dioecesana.* Romae, 1806.

BERLENDI, *Delle Oblazioni All'Altare.* Venetiis, 1736.

BINTERIM, *Denkwürdigkeiten des Christlichen Altertums.* Mainz, 1828.

BIBLE. New York, 1914.

BLAT, *Commentarium Textus Codicis Iuris Canonici.* Romae, 1920.

BONACINA, *Opera Omnia.* Lyons, 1684. *Tractatus De Sacramentis.*

CANONISTE CONTEMPORAIN. Louvain, 1917.

CAPPELLO, *Tractatus Canonico-Moralis De Sacramentis* (Vol. I). Romae, 1921.

CATHOLIC ENCYCLOPEDIA. New York, 1911.

DEL GIUDICE. *Stipendia Missarum.* Romae, 1922.

DE LA TAILLE, *Mysterium Fidei.* Parisiis, 1921.

DE LUGO, *De Sacramento Eucharistiae.* Lyons, 1651 resp. Parisiis, 1869.

DILLON, *Bequests for Masses.* Chicago, 1896.

DENZINGER, *Enchiridion Symbolorum.* Friburgi, 1922.

DIANA, *Theologia Moralis.* Venetiis, 1728.

FERRERES, *Las Misas Manuales.* Madrid, 1924.

GARDELLINI, *Decreta Authentica, S. R. C.* Romae, 1856.

GASPARRI, *De Eucharistia.* Parisiis, 1897.

GEIER, *De Missarum Stipendiis.* Moguntiae, 1864.

GENICOT-SALSMANS, *Theologia Moralis Institutiones.* Bruxellis, 1912.

GREGORIANUM (Vol. IV). Romae, 1923.

HILLING, *Die Mess-Stipendien und Stolgebühren.* Bonn, 1916.

HARDOUIN, *Acta Conciliorum.* Parisiis, 1714.

HERGENRÖTHER, *Kirchenlexikon.* Freiburg, 1887.

HOMILETIC AND PASTORAL REVIEWS. New York, 1921.

HOCEDEZ, *Les Honoraires de Messe* (apud Revue Theologique).

IRENAEUS, *Contra Haereses* (apud Migne).

IRISH ECCLESIASTICAL RECORD (Vol. 19). 1922.

LEECH, *A Comparative Study.* Washington, 1922.

LAYMANN, *Theologia Moralis.* Patavii, 1733.

LEHMKUHL, *Theologia Moralis.* Freiburg, 1884.

LINK, *Mess-Stipendien.* Regensburg, 1901.

LINZER QUARTALSCHRIFT. 1924.

MARX, *Lehrbuch der Kirchengeschichte.* Trier, 1908.

MIGNE, *Patrologia Latina.* Parisiis, 1847.

MIGNE, *Patrologia Graeca.* Parisiis, 1858.

MOREY, *Outlines of Roman Law.* New York, 1913.

MOTRY, *Diocesan Faculties.* Washington, 1922.

NOLDIN, *De Praeceptis.* Oeniponte, 1921.

NOLDIN, *De Sacramentis.* Oeniponte, 1923.

NOUVELLE REVUE THEOLOGIQUE. Louvain, 1923.

ORIGEN, *In Numeros Homilia* XI. (apud Migne).

PALLOTTINI, *Collectio Omnium Conclusionum et Resolutionum Sacrae Congregationis Concilii.* Romae, 1887.

PIGNATELLI, *Consultationes Cannonicae.* Venetiis, 1736.

PROBST, *Die Abendländische Messe vom Fünften bis zum Achten Jahrhundert.* Münster, 1896.

PRÜMMER, *Manuale Theologiae Moralis.* Freiburg, 1923.

RAYMOND DE PENNAFORT, *Summa,* Ed. Veronensis, 1744.

REVUE THEOLOGIQUE. Louvain, 1923.

REIFFENSTUEL, *Ius Canonicum Universum.* Venetiis, 1735.

SCHMALZGRUEBER, *Ius Ecclesiasticum Universum.*

SCOTUS, *Opera Omnia.* Parisiis, 1895.

SMITH, *Elements of Ecclesiastical Law.* New York, 1887.

SEBASTIANI, *Summarium Theologiae Moralis,* Ed. Quarta Minor.

SLATER, *Cases of Conscience.* New York, 1911 and 1912.

STATUTA PROVINCIALIA ET DIOECESANA. Philadelphiae, 1897.

SOLE, *De Delictis et Poenis.* Romae, 1920.

SUAREZ, *De Sacramento Eucharistiae.* Parisiis, 1866.

TANQUEREY, *Synopsis Theologiae Dogmaticae.* New York, 1920.

TELCH, *Epitome Theologiae Moralis.* Romae, 1919.

TERTULLIAN, *De Monogamia, Ad Uxorem, De Exhortatione Castitatis* (apud Migne).

VAN ESPEN, *Ius Ecclesiasticum Universum.* Venetiis, 1769.

VERMEERSCH-CREUSEN, *Epitome Iuris Canonici.* Romae, 1922.

WERNZ, *Ius Decretalium.* Romae, 1901.

WOYWOD, *The New Canon Law.* New York, 1918.

PREFACE

This dissertation treats of a topic that has the merit of being familiar, new, up-to-date, practical and interesting. Priests and laymen are quite familiar with the subject of Mass stipends or "money for Masses," as these offerings are often called. Yet no one seems to have written a monograph on this subject in English; and even in the foreign languages there is a noticeable dearth of books that treat professedly of stipends alone.

It is true that the pages which authors of general works on canon law and moral theology have written about these offerings suffice to fill a bookcase. But to collect this material into one manual; to bring such a digest up-to-date by indicating the changes which the Code has introduced into the matter and the form of the Church's laws concerning these contracts; to make this comparative study a practical explanation of the canons on stipends; to render this practical commentary more interesting by giving also the history and theories which form the background and substratum of the present legislation; and finally to couch this canonical lore in readable English; to do all this seems equivalent to making a trifling contribution to the sum of human knowledge.

To what extent the present work succeeds in doing this remains for the reader to judge. For the author, there remains only the pleasant duty of expressing his cordial gratitude to the Faculty of Canon Law for reading the manuscript and suggesting changes of practical moment.

CHAPTER I

RECEPTUM
OR
THE HISTORICAL ASPECT OF MASS STIPENDS

Although the Code is primarily a digest of laws, still it contains a considerable number of canons which are not laws in the strict sense of the word, but are rather explanations of terms or declarations of principles or vindications of rights. Thus one finds in Canon 824 an authentic declaration and vindication of a priest's right to accept compensation for saying and applying a Mass. These are the words of the canon: [1]

> "Secundum receptum et probatum Ecclesiae morem atque institutum, sacerdoti cuilibet Missam celebranti et applicanti licet eleemosynam seu stipendium recipere.
>
> "Quoties autem pluries in die celebrat, si unam Missam ex titulo justitiae applicet, sacerdos, praeterquam in die Nativitatis Domini, pro alia eleemosynam recipere nequit, excepta aliqua retributione ex titulo extrinseco."

Woywod's rendition of this canon is worded as follows: [2]

> "According to an established and approved custom of the Church, any priest who says and applies Holy Mass may receive an alms or stipend.
>
> "Whenever he says Holy Mass several times a day, and has to apply one Mass from a title of justice, he can not receive another stipend, excepting some compensation from an extrinsic title. On Christmas, however, he may receive a stipend also for the second and third Mass."

1 Codex Juris Canonici, canon 824.

2 Woywod, The New Canon Law, par. 667, p. 166.

It may be well to give a preliminary definition of Mass stipends at the very beginning of the treatise. A Mass stipend is a sum of money which is given to a priest for applying the special fruit of a Mass celebrated by him. Or, as Vermeersch says,[3] "Stipendium, seu eleemosyna Missarum est res pretio aestimabilis, plerumque pecunia, quae solvitur sacerdoti promittenti ex justitia applicationem."

In the first section of Canon 824, there are four words which may serve as basic notes for the four themes which they respectively suggest. The word "receptum" suggests the history of Mass stipends. The verb "licet" strikes the keynote of stipends considered theologically. "Probatum" is the theme of stipends in their canonical aspect. Lastly, the synonyms "eleemosynam seu stipendium" evoke a brief etymological consideration of the various names which have been applied to these offerings at various times and with varying degrees of precision. An essay on stipends, therefore, should show first of all that the giving and receiving of Mass stipends has been for centuries an established usage.

After the Ascension of our Lord, the Apostles and the rest of the faithful, whose number before Pentecost was 120,[4] continued living and eating in common. In Jerusalem, the Apostles depended for their sustenance upon the offerings of those faithful. One may assume that, as a consequence of their community life, the Apostles celebrated the Eucharistic Supper after their usual evening meal, thus imitating the example and obeying the precept of their Divine Master,[5] "Do this for a commemoration of me."

Later, those faithful who could not attend the divine services on weekdays were present at the supper on Sundays; and the taking of the meal in common was soon transferred from the original cenaculum to the so-

3 Vermeersch, Epitome iuris Canonici, Vol. II, p. 51, n. 103.

4 Acts I, 13-15.

5 Luke xxii, 19.

called house-churches.[6] This banquet was a manifestation of Christian unity, and later it was called an Agape or love feast.

As the congregation increased, the daily love feast with daily Communion became impossible; and in its stead there came weekly Communion on Sundays and the Agape in the strict sense of the term. The Agape was no longer an ordinary meal for the sustenance of human life, but a banquet symbolic of the Christian Communion and affording an opportunity of feeding the poor. This Agape used to take place in the house-churches at the time when St. Paul wrote his first Epistle to the Christians of Corinth, *i. e.*, about Easter, A. D. 57.[7] Finally, because of the abuses attendant upon it the Agape was prohibited in the fourth century.[8]

Closely connected with the Agape were the offerings of the faithful; for these offerings alone made the love feasts possible. The notable offerings made by those Christians of Jerusalem who sold their possessions and gave the proceeds to the Apostles, are in proportion with the great expense which the community life entailed.

However, one must distinguish between those offerings which were given in charity for the poor at the love feasts and the other offerings of bread and wine, which latter gifts were changed by Consecration into the Body and Blood of Christ and then given back to their donors in Holy Communion. This distinction between eucharistic and non-eucharistic offerings was made in apostolic times.

Turning from this Biblical lore of the first century to the tradition recorded in the writings of the Fathers, one learns from St. Irenaeus, who flourished towards the close of the second century, that God prescribed an offer-

6 Acts ii, 46.

7 I Cor. xi, 20-22.

8 Alzog, Universalgeschichte, Vol. I, p. 217. "Bedauernswerthe Missbräuche veranlassten die Synoden im vierten Jahrh. zum gänzlichen Verbote derselben."

ing which should be placed upon the altar and offered frequently, nay uninterruptedly.[9]

Tertullian (born 160 A. D.), writing to a widower who wanted to marry again, asked this significant question:[10] "You pray for your deceased wife and offer the annual sacrifice for her. But if you marry again, will you offer sacrifice for the two wives and recommend both of them to God through the priest?" The writer uses expressions such as "You make yearly offerings; *you* offer for two wives; will your sacrifice ascend?" The words "Your sacrifice" point definitely to the man who has made the priest's Mass his own sacrifice by requesting its celebration and excluding others from its special application. The expression "oblationes annuas reddis" refers in all probability to an Anniversary Mass of Requiem;[11] and it is repeated in another passage. A third sentence from this second century author inclines us to think that a similar offering was made to the priest or bishop, not by the faithful in general, but by the contracting parties at the celebration of the Eucharist on the occasion of a wedding, *i. e.*, at a Nuptial Mass.[13]

9 Irenaeus, Contra Haereses, Liber IV, caput VIII ad finem: "Sicut igitur non his indigens vult tamen a nobis propter nos fieri, ne simus infructuosi: ita ad ipsum Verbum populo praeceptum faciendarum oblationum, quamvis non indiget eis, ut discerent Deo servire; sic et ideo nos quoque offerre vult munus ad altare frequenter sine intermissione." M. P. G., VII, 1029.

10 Tertullian, De Exhortatione Castitatis, caput XI. "Duplex enim rubor est; quia in secundo matrimonio duae uxores eumdem circumstant maritum; una spiritu, alia in carne: neque enim pristinam poteris odisse, cui etiam religiosiorem reservas affectionem, ut jam receptae apud Dominum, pro cujus spiritu postulas, pro qua oblationes annuas reddis. Stabis ergo ad Dominum cum tot uxoribus quot in oratione commemoras? Et offeres pro duabus? Et commendabis illas duas per sacerdotem de monogamia ordinatum, aut etiam de virginitate sancitum, circumdatum virginibus a univiris, et ascendet sacrificium tuum libera fronte? et inter caeteras voluntates bonae mentis, postulabis tibi et uxori castitatem?" M. P. L., II, 926.

11 Tertullian, De Monogamia, caput X. "Enim vero et pro anima ejus orat, et refrigerium interim adpostulat ei, et in prima resurrectione consortium, et offert annuis diebus dormitionis ejus." M. P. L., II, 942-c.

13 Tertullian, Ad Uxorem, Liber II, caput IX. "Unde sufficiamus ad enarrandam felicitatem ejus matrimonii, quod Ecclesia conciliat, et *confirmat oblatio*, et obsignat benedictio, angeli renuntiant, Pater rato habet." M. P. L., I, 1302.

Origen (185-254) mentions offerings which consist of victuals and money.[14]

In the middle of the sixth century, the Ultragothic wife of King Childebert made many offerings for Masses in honor of St. Martin.[15] Towards the close of the same century, Pope Gregory I declared that one-fourth of the sacrificial bread presented by the faithful belonged to the clergy.[16] About that time, the offering of bread was going into desuetude.[17]

Even Van Espen admits that when the offering of bread ceased, the person who wished to have a Mass said used to give the priest a piece of money.[18]

Treating of the seventh century, Venerable Bede tells us that people used to have Masses said for their intentions by priests to whom they gave money for that purpose.[19] Likewise, St. John the Almoner, who was Bishop of Alexandria from 610 to 616, offered Holy Mass for the safe return of a son whose father had given money to the Bishop for saying Mass for that intention.[20]

According to the rule of St. Chrodegang, an individual priest was permitted in the eighth century to

14 Origen, In Numeros Homilia XI, n. 9. "Sed rursus muneris offert primitias, si non solum cibos, verbi gratia, vel pecuniam largiatus, sed et affectum miserendi habeat, et compatiendi." M. P. G., XII, 655.

15 Cf. Migne P. L., LXXI, col. 926.

16 Gregory I, Liber XIII, Epistola 44; apud Migne P. L., LXXVII, 1293.

17 Probst, Die Abendländische Messe, p. 328.

18 Van Espen, Jus Eccl., tom. 1, p. 2, tit. 5. De Celebr. Missae, c. 5, n. 1. "Dum jam sensim Oblatio inter Missarum solemnia pene cessaret, atque in Missis praecipue privatis Oblatio parum nota esset, tunc qui pro se specialiter tanquam Offerente Missam celebrari, et orari volebat id oblato denario a Sacerdote postulabat atque hinc ille denarius quem hodie Honorarium, aut Stipendium vocamus."

19 Bede, Historia Anglorum, lib. IV, c. 22, Migne P. L., XCV, col. 205-207.

20 Cappello, De Sacramentis, Vol. I, p. 527, n. 661.

receive an alms in return for a Mass applied for the donor or his loved ones.[21]

In the ninth century, Walafrid Strabo [22] attacked the application of a Mass's special fruit to any individual (and consequently the reception of stipends), on the ground that a man who gave the alms could not profit by the Mass anymore than the rest of the faithful. St. Matilda, the wife of King Henry I of Germany, lived in the middle of the tenth century. Of her it is said that she took two bracelets off of her arms; and giving them to a priest, said to him, "Accipe tibi hoc aurum, et canta Missam Animarum" ("Take this gold and sing a Requiem Mass").[23]

A story is told about St. Peter Damien, who lived in the eleventh century. One day this saint, when still a boy, found a coin and rejoiced in his riches. But, being inspired from on high, he exclaimed, " 'Tis better that I give it to a priest, who will offer the Sacrifice to God for my father." [24] In a biography of St. Bertold, who died at the close of the twelfth century, we read that a man of God showed a coin to a newly ordained priest and asked for a remembrance in his First Mass.[25]

The thirteenth, "the greatest of centuries," brings to us the sad story of the Missa Sicca. John Eck, Luther's adversary, informs us: [26] "Missam Siccam appellant; quando Die Dominico, aut Festo Sacerdos simulat omnia, quae sunt Celebrantis cum Introitu, Collecta, Epistola, Evangelio, et Canticis; tamen quia non habet communicantem, nec ipse vult communicare, ideo non consecrat;

21 "Regula Chrodegangi; Si quis uni Sacerdoti pro Missa sua, seu pro seipso, vel pro quolibet caro suo, aut vivente, aut mortuo, aliquid in eleemosyna dare voluerit, hoc Sacerdos a tribuente accipiat, et exinde quod voluerit, faciat." Chrodegangi, Regula Canonicorum, c. XLII, M. P. L., LXXXIX, col. 1076.

22 Walafrid Strabo, De Rebus Eccl., cap. 22, quoted by Benedict XIV, Cf. M. P. L, 114, col. 951.

23 Berlendi, Delle Oblazioni, p. 280.

24 Benedict XIV, De Missae Sacrificio, p. 223.

25 Berlendi, Delle Oblazioni, p. 259.

26 Eck, Annot, ad lib. Oblat. Caesari, art. 21. Quoted by Berlendi, Delle Oblazioni, p. 287.

sed est Missa Sicca, sine Eucharistia, sine Corpore et Sanguine Christi."

The Council of Paris, held in 1212 and presided over by Cardinal Robert, the papal legate, formulated this canon: [27] "Prohibemus ne pro annualibus, vel triennalibus, vel septenannalibus Missarum faciendis Laici vel alii dare aliquid, vel legare in testamento cogantur, et ne super his aliqua pactio, vel actio vera, vel sub aliqua alia specie palliata a Sacerdotibus, vel aliis mediatoribus fiat, et ne superflua multitudine talium annalium se onerent Sacerdotes, propter quae ipsos oportet habere conductitios Sacerdotes; vel ut se exonerent, Siccas Missas faciant pro Defunctis." The reason for the Missa Sicca is given by Benedict XIV,[28] "quae omnia propter nefariam augendae pecuniae cupiditatem fieri consueverunt."

Akin to the Missa Sicca are the "Missae Bifaciatae" et "Missae Trifaciatae." "They consisted in this, that the celebrant would read the Introit, etc., to the Offertory; then he would read the canon once and for all; finally, he would add as many Postcommunions as he had recited Orations." Concerning this practice, Peter Cantor, who lived in Paris during the twelfth century, wrote these stinging words,[29] "Turpius Christum vendimus quam Judas . . . Ille pro triginta argenteis, nos pro denario, et pretio vilissimo."

The Missae Bifaciatae were celebrated most frequently in France; they were combated principally by Peter Cantor; and they disappeared about the year 1560. Reformatory laws against the Missae Bifaciatae were passed by the Synod of Paris in the year 1245; [30] and by the Synod of Worcester in 1240.[31]

27 Berlendi, Delle Oblazioni, p. 289.

28 Benedict XIV, Institutionum Eccl., Inst. LVI, n. II.

29 Peter Cantor, Verbum Abbreviatum, cap. 37. Quoted by Benedict XIV, Inst. LVI, n. II.

30 Hardouin, Conciliorum Coll., Vol. VI, Pars. II, col. 1940. "Nullus [Presbyter] bis in die audeat celebrare aut cum duplici Introitu."

31 Martene, Thesaur, nov. Anecd. tom. 4, p. 893; Hardouin, VI, II, p. 1940; Link, p. 136.

To continue the history of Mass stipends beyond the thirteenth century would be a mere waste of time; for the abuses just mentioned prove that the custom was well established at that time. It would be more advisable to summarize the transition from the primitive oblations to the modern stipends, and then to consider the answers which various authors have given to the question, "When did the custom of giving Mass stipends originate?"

The transition from the oblations of the early Christians to the Mass stipends of present-day Catholics comprised five distinct stages.

First stage: The people presented the eucharistic elements of bread and wine for Consecration. Before the close of the fourth century, the laymen themselves brought these gifts to the altar.[33] Then the celebrant of the Mass, in the presence of these people, changed the eucharistic elements by the words of Consecration into the substance of Christ's Body and Blood. In the Memento, *i. e.*, in the application of the Mass's fruits, the celebrant included all the faithful who had presented the bread and wine.[34] Finally the people who had contributed at the Offertory and had assisted devoutly at the Consecration received Holy Communion under one or both species. As late as the close of the sixth century, the Council of Macon (Canon 4) urged every man to bring with him the bread and wine required for his Communion.[35] This bread and wine, offered at the altar and intended primarily for Consecration and Communion, constituted the "Oblationes communes ad altare."

Second stage: As the Agape differed from the Mass, so did the offerings made at the love feast differ from the offerings made at the Lord's Supper. The offerings which were made at the Agape consisted largely of bread and wine; but other foodstuffs and even money were

33 Probst, Die Abenländische Messe, p. 273.

34 Link, Mess-Stipendien, pp. 28-31.

35 Probst, Die Abendländische Messe, p. 328, "Erubescere debet homo idoneus si de aliena oblatione communicaverit." M. P. L., Vol. XXXIX, p. 2, col. 2238.

donated.[36] "The faithful then brought their gifts of bread and wine; and in the earlier ages, the first fruits, or the one-sixtieth part of the crop, were part of their offering, and received the blessing of the bishop." These offerings were destined partly for the love feast itself, partly for the poor and partly for the clergy.[38] In the year 563, the Spanish Synod of Braga (Canon 22) decreed that the offerings made by the faithful should be collected by the archdeacon and distributed among the clergy annually or semi-annually.[39] He portioned out one part to the bishop, another to the priest and deacons, and the rest to the clerics of inferior rank. Pope Gregory the Great (510-604) tells that one-fourth of the bread presented by the faithful belonged to the clergy.[40]

These offerings constituted the "oblationes communes ad gazophylacium." This gazophylacium was nothing more than a receptacle for all kinds of donations. These gifts were not intended primarily for Consecration or Communion; they consisted, not of bread and wine alone, but of other edibles and money as well; and they were presented, not at the altar during Mass, but outside of Mass and at the gazophylacium or "poor-box." [41] Thus, as Binterim notes, panis terrestris or ordinary bread is distinguished from panis coelestis or eucharistic bread.[42] At this stage, all the participants in the fruits of the Mass were present at the essential action of the Mass (*i. e.*, the Consecration) and received Holy Communion; but they did not take part in the offertory.

Third stage: The third epoch in the evolution of Mass stipends may be illustrated with an anecdote related by St. Gregory of Tours.[43] For a whole year, a certain widow used to assist daily at Mass, which was celebrated

36 Origen, In Numeros Homilia XI, n. 9. M. P. G., XII, 655.

38. St. Cyprian Epistle 66, M. P. L., Vol. IV, col. 399; Cf. Noldin, III, n. 183.

39 Probst, Die Abendländische Messe, p. 414.

40 Epistle 44, M. P. L., Vol. LXXVII, col. 1295.

41 Link, Mess-Stipendien, p. 59.

42 Binterim, Denkwürdigkeiten, Vol. 4, part 3, p. 370.

43 Gregory of Tours, De Gloria Confessorum, cap. 65, M. P. L., LXXI, 875.

for her former husband, and, as her offering for the sacrifice, she was wont to give a "sextarium Gazeti vini," or in modern parlance, a pint of excellent wine. A nefarious subdeacon, however, used to reserve the good wine for his own palate, and substituted vinegar for the wine used at Mass. Admonished in a dream, the lady received Holy Communion the next morning at Mass; but to her horror she drank from the chalice "vinegar so sour that she thought her teeth were being knocked out."

From this story, Binterim infers:[44]

(a) That the daily Masses in question were private Masses and were attended by the widow alone; for otherwise some of the people present would have gone to Holy Communion and detected the fraud;

(b) That the widow brought the wine to the sacristy or to the priest's house; for otherwise the subdeacon could not have substituted the vinegar for the wine;

(c) That the widow who offered the wine did not go to Holy Communion frequently.

In other words, the giver of the offering at this period no longer took part in the Offertory or the Communion, but only in the Consecration or sacrifice itself by attending Mass and having its fruits offered for her deceased husband. From the earliest times, the eucharistic elements at Masses for the Dead had not been offered at those Masses by the mourners, because the mourners did not receive Holy Communion at the Requiem. A part of the eucharistic offerings were often mingled with the non-eucharistic oblations; and were consigned to the gazophylacium; and from this source were supplied the bread and wine which were consecrated at the Mass of Requiem.[45]

Fourth stage: Hence it was natural that the mourners made up for the lack of eucharistic offerings by giving money instead of bread and wine. From the very beginning, money had been offered occasionally at Masses for

44 Binterim, Denkwürdigkeiten, Vol. 4, part 3, p. 373.

45 Link, Mess-Stipendien, p. 28.

the Dead.[46] Even at Masses for the Living, one or another of the faithful preferred to give money rather than bread and wine.

In the early centuries of the Christian era, the regular Mass was the Solemn Mass; but private Masses were quite common in the seventh century.[47] As the private Masses grew in frequency, so too did the pecuniary offerings.[48] These general offerings (oblationes communes ad manum) were not stipends in the modern or strict sense of the term. Perhaps the Masses which were said for such offerings were more akin to the Missa Pro Populo and the Masses which are offered up for the benefactors of seminaries, orphanages, etc.

Fifth stage: Mass stipends in the strict sense are termed oblationes particulares. They differ from all other offerings (oblationes communes ad altare, oblationes communes ad gazophylacium) in these three respects: first, Mass stipends are given, morally speaking, by an individual person to an individual priest; second, the giver gets an exclusive right in justice to all the special fruits of the Mass; and third, the giver of the Mass stipend need not be present at the Offertory, Consecration or Communion of the Mass for which he has given the stipend. As Communion of the laity became less frequent, less bread and wine were needed for Mass; and gradually money was given in their stead to supply all the needs of the celebrant.[50] But the date when pecuniary offerings outnumbered the sacrificial oblations can not be determined.[51] Still more difficult would be the attempt to fix precisely the date on which the first Mass stipend in the technical meaning of the term was given to a priest.

Wernz says that the usage certainly existed in the

46 Link, Mess-Stipendien, p. 58.

47 Marx, Universalgeschichte, p. 331.

48 Catholic Encyclopedia, art. Mass., Vol. X, p. 21.

50 Binterim, Denkwürdigkeiten, Vol. 4, part. 3, p. 378.

51 Benedict XIV, De Synodo, lib. V, cap. 8.

eighth century; [52] that it became much more general during the eleventh century; and that authorities admit its universality in the twelfth century. Van Espen said that stipends came into vogue during the ninth century, when private Masses superseded the Solemn Mass.[53] Marx states that this transition took place before the seventh century, at which time private Masses seem to have been quite common.[54]

It seems that Mass stipends in the strict sense of the term existed before the eighth century.[55] Beyond this, "it cannot be stated with certainty when the custom developed to make an offering for Holy Mass to the individual priest; in fact, it would be historically wrong to assign a fixed date to early customs of the Church, for it is precisely the nature of a practice introduced by custom that it rises gradually and, if considered lawful, spreads steadily until it becomes universal in the Church." [56]

To conclude: A canonist may learn from history that the sacrificial oblations in their metamorphosis have passed through the forms called the oblationes communes ad altare, the oblationes communes ad gazophylacium, the oblationes communes ad manum, before emerging into the oblationes particulares or formal stipend; and still he can consistently believe that the modern Mass stipend differs essentially from the primeval offerings from which it has developed.[57].

52 Wernz, Jus Decretalium, Vol. III, n. 537: "Quae praxis veri stipendii saltem saeculo octavo fuit recepta; . . . multo magis autem ex saeculo undecimo et duodecimo est divulgata."

53 Van Espen, Jus Eccl. tom. 1, p. 2, tit, 5, c 5.

54 Marx, Lehrbuch der Kirchengeschichte, p. 331.

55 E. Hocedez, "Les Honoraires de Messe," in Revue Theologique, Tome 50me, p. 70.

56 Woywod, art. "The Regulation, etc.," sub-title "Mass Stipends," The Homiletic & Pastoral Reviews, Vol. XXI, p. 805.

57 Cf. A. K. K., 1892, Vol. 68, p. 266.

CHAPTER II

THEOLOGICAL ASPECT OF MASS STIPENDS

This introduction facilitates the proving of the thesis, that it is lawful for any priest who celebrates and applies a Mass to accept a stipend. Needless to say, arguments in favor of this proposition are drawn from Scripture, tradition and reason. From the Bible, theologians quote the following texts: "The workman is worthy of his meat." [1] "The laborer is worthy of his hire." [2] "Who serveth as a soldier, at any time at his own charges. . . . If we have sown unto you spiritual things, is it a great matter if we reap your carnal things? . . . Know you not that they who work in the holy places eat the things that are of the holy place; and they that serve the altar partake with the altar?" [3]

A moment's reflection will convince the reader that these texts have but little value. At most, they prove that by divine law the Church has the right to demand from the faithful the maintenance of her clergy.[4] But they do not prove that the individual who asks for the application of a Mass must give the priest a sum of money.

Nor will pure reason supply an apodictical argument. Natural law, it is true, binds the faithful in a general way to support those who minister to their spiritual needs; for no one is bound to serve others gratuitously. Nevertheless, this general obligation does not demonstrate the liceity of Mass stipends any more than it proves that the people should give money for indulgences, absolution or Extreme Unction. Again, someone might

1 Matt. x, 10.
2 Luke x, 7.
3 I Cor. ix, 7-14, "Quis militat suis stipendiis unquam?"
4 Cf. Cornelly, in I Cor. ix, 12-14.

attempt to justify the taking of stipends with the plea that the only effective way of curtailing requests, reasonable or unreasonable, for the application of Masses, is to demand a sum of money as a condition for granting the request, but not as an equivalent of the Mass itself. But a polite refusal or a mental reservation would be just as effective. No; Scripture and reason may furnish confirmatory arguments, but they do not demonstrate the thesis, which can be proven apodictically from one source only, viz.: tradition. The cogency of the argument from tradition contrasts favorably with the arguments from the two other sources: its strength is proportionate to their weakness.

First, the giving and receiving of Mass stipends is a usage which, as was seen in the first chapter, dates back at least twelve hundred years. Moreover, the Church has not only tolerated this usage by not reproving it, but has actually approved the practice by issuing numerous decrees concerning it. The point is this: the Church cannot make any universal law contrary to the natural or positive divine law. But the Church has made numerous laws in favor of Mass stipends; and in the Council of Trent it went so far as to empower the bishops to fix the amount of money which their priests might lawfully demand.[5]

Consequently, Mass stipends must be lawful. Abuses, indeed, are unlawful, and the Church has condemned them more than once. But the thing itself the Church has never condemned. Far from condemning the practice, the Church has condemned several errors opposed to it, such as the errors of Wycliff and the pseudo-council of Pistoja. Any lingering doubt about the Church's attitude towards Mass stipends is dispelled by the Code itself, through Canon 824. There one finds the simple and unequivocal declaration, "Any priest who says and applies Holy Mass may receive an alms or stipend." [5b]

5 Trent, Sess. XXII, de observandis. (Richter, p. 136) p. 140.

5[b] Woywod, "The New Canon Law," p. 166, n. 667.

The reader is now prepared to consider the most difficult topic, viz.: the nature of Mass stipends. This topic resolves itself into three questions:

(1) Does the giving and acceptance of Mass stipends constitute a contract?

(2) Why is it a mortal sin to omit a single Mass promised in return for a stipend?

(3) Are stipends simoniacal?

A contract is said to be an agreement between two or more persons to do or forbear something legal, or an agreement concerning a transfer of rights.[6] A valid contract requires:[7] suitable subject matter, capable persons, mutual consent and reason for the consent.

The giving and acceptance of a Mass stipend squares with all these requirements. The capable persons, mutual consent and reason for the consent are evident. As regards the subject-matter, a careless person might remark that the priest says a Mass and receives a sum of money. But to be precise, it must be said that the person who gives the offering transfers to the priest the right to a sum of money for the celebrant's sustenance, and in return the priest gives to that person a right to the special fruit of the Mass applied by the priest to that person's intention.

Mass stipends belong to that class of bilateral innominate contracts which is known as "do ut facias." This means that one party agrees to give something whilst the other party agrees to do something in return. To confirm this assertion, read these words of Woywod,[8] "For in a bilateral contract, do stipendium ut applices Missam ad meam intentionem, the obligation should be equally grave for both contracting parties."

In the ultimate analysis, the priest agrees to do something, viz.: to apply the Mass, as the Code insinuates by

6 Vermeersch-Creusen, Epitome Juris Canonici, Vol. II, p. 458, n. 849: "Contractus definitur duorum vel plurium in idem placitum juris consensus."

7 Noldin, Summa Theol. Moralis, Vol. II, De Praeceptis, p. 542, n. 523. "Contractus definiri potest: duorum vel plurium de jure transferendo consensus."

8 The Homiletic & Pastoral Reviews, 1921, Vol. XXI, p. 923.

using the active participle, "applicanti." [9] At any rate, the intrinsic nature of Mass stipends as explained in the preceding pages and the extrinsic authority of Vermeersch, Woywod and Benedict XIV, are sufficient reasons for not accepting Cappello's [10] theory that Mass stipends are only quasi-contracts, but not contracts in the strict sense of the term.

Woywod [11] calls attention to the fact that the Code uses the word "obligation" instead of "contract," because in this matter the agreement between the priest and the donor is implicit, not explicit. But in using this general expression, the authors of the Code are simply adhering to their policy of not solving debatable questions of a theoretical nature.

Mass stipends bespeak a strict contract which belongs to the innominate species. This is fraught with significant consequences. The first of these consequences is the corollary that Mass stipends do not come under the heading of contracts of sale (contractus emptionis-venditionis).[12] The second corollary is that there need not be any proportion between the value of the stipend and the value of the Mass.[12]

The third consequence of this theory solves the second question proposed on page 25, viz.: Why is it a mortal sin to omit even one Mass promised for a stipend? The answer to the question and the consequence of the theory is this: In virtue of his innominate contract, the priest is bound in commutative justice and under penalty of mortal sin to apply the Mass according to the intention of the person who gave the stipend.[13] The priest's serious obligation arises, not primarily from canon law

9 Canon 824.

10 Cappello, De Sacramentis, Vol. I, p. 535, n. 668.

11 The Homiletic and Pastoral Reviews, Vol. XXI, p. 807.

12 Vermeersch-Creusen, Epitome J. C., Vol. II, p. 5, n. 8. "Contractus quo pro eo (stipendio) opus spirituale promittitur non est venditionis vel locationis, sed innominatus: Do ut facias, quod nullam exigit aequalitatem vel comparationem inter id quod datur et illud quod fiet, cum aliunde, v. g. ex indigentia accipientis, quid congruum sit aestimari possit."

13 Vermeersch-Creusen, Epitome J. C., Vol. II, p. 54, n. 106.

nor from the monetary or exchange value of the stipend, but from the contract itself as regulated by ecclesiastical law.[14]

For the priest who accepts a stipend agrees to do something very important for the other person, viz.: to apply to him the priceless fruit of Holy Mass. This agreement is not a mere unilateral promise; for the celebrant of the Mass accepts money from the other person. But even if the priest were bound by reason of his promise alone, he could and he actually does promise to say that Mass ex justitia. Consequently, if the priest breaks the promise which binds him in justice to do something for the giver of the stipend, that priest causes the other person a serious loss or injury; and therefore, commits a mortal sin.

Finally, the fourth consequence of the principle gives the lie to the assertion that Mass stipends are simoniacal. Simony is either of divine law or of ecclesiastical law.[15] Mass stipends do not constitute simony of ecclesiastical law, because the Church, far from forbidding them, expressly permits them,[16] and in stipends there is no simony of divine law, because they do not imply any will to buy or sell, as was explained on page 26. They express a mere agreement by the one party to give something and by the other party to do something.

14 Canon 828, "Tot celebrandae et applicandae sunt Missae, quot stipendia etiam exigua data et accepta fuerint." Cf. Woywod, art. "Mass Stipends" in Homiletic & Pastoral Review, Vol. XXI, p. 923.

15 Canon 727, "Studiosa voluntas emendi vel vendendi pro pretio temporali rem intrinsece spiritualem . . . vel rem temporalem rei spirituali adnexam ita ut res temporalis sine spirituali nullo modo esse possit,. . . aut res spiritualis sit objectum, etsi partiale, contractus, . . . est simonia juris divini."

"Dare vero res temporales spirituali adnexas pro temporalibus spirituali adnexis, vel res spirituales pro spiritualibus, vel etiam temporales pro temporalibus, si id ob periculum irreverentiae erga res spirituales ab Ecclesia prohibeatur, est simonia juris ecclesiastici."

16 Cf. Canon 824—1.

St. Thomas Aquinas [17] says that Mass stipends are not simoniacal, because the priest accepts them as a payment of his sustenance, but not as the price of his Mass. De Lugo [18] makes use of a comparison: An artist, he says, makes a vow to paint gratuitously a masterpiece for a certain church. But whilst he is painting the picture, the artist demands not only a sum of money for the colors and other materials, but even the price of his board and lodging. Now moralists teach that such an artist does not commit a sin against his vow by demanding the payment of his expenses; and they claim that in spite of such demands the artist must be said to be painting gratis. In like manner, the priest accepts or even demands a partial payment of his expenses; but he does not accept a paltry piece of money as the price or monetary equivalent of the spiritual favors conferred through the application of the Mass.

Arendt, however, excoriates the plagiarists who slavishly repeat the argument of St. Thomas; and he says that they fall into the very simony which they are trying to explain away.[19] Scotus considered Mass stipends a reciprocity of gratuitous donations.[20] Slightly different from Scotus' concept is the opinion of Pignatelli, who thought that stipends, though they did not constitute a contract, were something more than donations, because they imposed a mutual obligation upon the giver of the money and the celebrant of the Mass.[21] Noel Alexander [22] and Van Espen [23] deny that any causal nexus exists between the money and the Mass.

17 St. Thomas Aquinas, Summa Theologica, 2—2, q. 100, art. 2, ad 2. "Ad secundum dicendum, quod Sacerdos non accipit pecuniam, quasi pretium consecrationis Eucharistiae, aut Missae decantandae (hoc enim esset simoniacum); sed quasi stipendium suae sustentationis, ut dictum est (in corp.)."

18 Le Lugo, De Sacramento Eucharistiae, Disputatio XXI, Vol. IV, p. 275, Parisiis, 1869.

19 Arendt, De laesione justitiae, etc., n. 21, n. 41.

20 Scotus, Quaestiones Quodlibetales, Quaest XX, n. 25; Vol. 26, p. 324. Del Giudice, p. 46.

21 Pignatelli Consultationes Canonicae, Tom. IV, cons. 227.

22 Cf. Noel Alexander, Theol. Dogm. et Mor., lib 2, De Simonia, reg. 35, p. 523.

23 Cf. Van Espen, Jus Eccl. Universum, Tom. I, pars. 2, sect. 1, tit. 5, cap. 6, n. 1.

Bonacina taught that priests might accept stipends because they were thus demanding nothing more than their support from their employers; "qui negotia alterius gerit potest substentationem ab eo exigere." [24]

Mostazo, a jurist of the sixteenth century, proposed an explanation which is still popular. According to him, priests can not engage in other lucrative pursuits during the time that it takes them to say Mass. Now, as a rule, no priest is obliged to say Mass for the special intention of any other person. Hence, the people who ask for this special ministration to their spiritual desires are bound by natural, divine and human law to make a special contribution towards the support of the priest who applies the Mass according to their intention.[25] Four centuries later, a similar explanation was given in the American Ecclesiastical Review.[26]

Laymann thought that the Mass stipend is given for the service which the priest performs in favor of the other person. His opinion seems to be based on the principle that "one good turn deserves another." He claims that the money is given, non in ordine ad opus spirituale, sed in ordine ad operantem. Laymann's hypothesis seems to besmirch a Mass stipend with the taint of simony; for it represents the priest as accepting money for the labor inseparably connected with the celebration of Mass, *i. e.*, for a res temporalis concomitanter et intrinsece spirituali connexa.[27]

De La Taille proposed the novel theory that the celebrant of the Mass is not remunerated by the layman, but is sustained by God. To him the Mass stipend is a sacred thing, like the lamb which had been consecrated to God by being offered on the altar of the Old Law. Hence, as the Jewish priest who ate a portion of the sacrificial lamb partook of something sacred, so does

24 Cf. Bonaeina, Tract. de Sacramentis, Disputatio IV; Cf. Del Giudice, Stipendia Missarum, p. 122.

25 Cf. Mostazo, Tractatus de Causis Piis, liber II, Tract. de Missis, de stipendiis etc.; cap. XII, Cf. Del Giudice, pp. 131-133.

26 Cf. Amer. Eccl. Review, Vol. 39, year 1908, pp. 234 sqq.

27 Laymann, Theol. Moralis, l. 4, Tract 10, cap. 8, 4, n. 41.

the Catholic priest partake of sacred food purchased with a gift from God.[28]

Del Giudice, a contemporary writer on Mass stipends, rejects the theory of the innominate contract and exonerates the person who asks for a Mass from any obligation of giving the stipend ex justitia. He proposes as his conviction the opinion that a contract for Masses constitutes a mandate.[29] This means that the celebrant of the Mass is simply the agent who offers the Holy Sacrifice as the giver of the stipend has asked him to do. Since the offering of money is not considered to be the priest's pay, the mandate is a unilateral, gratuitous contract, which is perfected by the mere consent of the sacerdotal agent.

In other words, Del Giudice admits that a true contract exists between the giver of the stipend and the celebrant of the Mass; but he denies that this contract is bilateral. His denial rests on the assertions that the priest cannot be compelled to say the Mass and that the giver of a stipend has no other assurance than the priest's own word concerning the application of the Mass. Now, in point of fact, it is a matter of common knowledge that every Ordinary can punish with coercive penalties his priests who would dare to keep a stipend without applying the corresponding Mass.[30] Del Giudice's second reason for saying that the contract in question is not bilateral is summed up in the statement that the priest's activity has no economic value, and consequently cannot form the subject matter of a bilateral contract which binds in commutative justice. It is evident, however, that even though the fruit of the Mass is beyond evaluation, still the honorarium of the Mass has a very definite economic or market value, viz.: the diocesan stipend which is fixed by law or custom. Del Giudice, then, has failed to disprove the contention of so many

28 Cf. De La Taille, "Les Offrandes De Messe," in Gregorianum, anno IV, Vol. IV, fasc. 3, September, 1923, ad Summarium in fine.

29 Cf. Del Giudice, Stipendia Missarum, p. 143.

30 Cf. Canon 2222 and 2324.

other canonists, that Mass stipends give rise to bilateral contracts.

In fact, almost every author who has written on this subject seems to have excogitated his own hypothesis; and so a mere enumeration of all these vagaries would fill a volume.[31] But the most common, as well as the most satisfactory, explanation of the nature of Mass stipends is the theory of the innominate contract, which was proposed by Suarez [32] and defended by Gasparri.[33]

31 Cf. Del Giudice, Stipendia Missarum, pp. 31-142.

32 Cf. Suarez, De Sacramento Eucharistiae; disp. 86, sect. 1, "Intervenit ergo ibi vera ratio justitiae fundata in mutuo consensu utrinque oneroso, qui explicatur illis verbis, do ut facias. Hic est autem titulus justitiae."

33 Cf. Gasparri, Tract. can. de Sacramento Eucharistia, Vol. I, p. 394. "Est inter sacerdotem et fidelem contractus innominatus, do ut facias."

CHAPTER III

ELEEMOSYNAM
OR
THE ETYMOLOGICAL ASPECT OF MASS STIPENDS

The experts who drafted the Code of Canon Law wavered in their choice of a word to designate the offering made to a priest for the application of a Mass. In Canon 824, and throughout the title, the terms "eleemosyna" and "stipendium" are used as synonyms. In Canon 827 we find the phrase, "A stipe Missarum." Formerly, the word "honorarium" expressed the same idea; and from it is derived the term still used by the French, "Les Honoraires de Messe." These various expressions deserve at least a brief consideration.

The Latin noun "oblationes" and its English derivative "oblations," are not used when referring to Mass stipends. Sometimes they mean an offering made to a church, but not directly to and for the priest. They are applied generally to the offering of the eucharistic elements, bread and wine; and in this sense, "Oblationes" or "oblations" are opposed to the stipends or offerings of money for the support of the clergy.

The word "offering" (not "oblation") is gaining favor among priests and laymen. It recalls to mind the fact that the stipend has superseded the primitive "offering." It is theologically unobjectionable; it has no offensive connotation; and, above all, it is simple enough for anyone to understand and use. The only objection to the word "offering" is the fact that this term is generic and does not distinguish a Mass stipend from a baptismal fee or a block collection.

Eleemosyna is a Greek word derived from " ελεέω " (to have pity on), and it means an act of relieving the needy or anything bestowed in charity.[1] From it are

1 Cf. Liddell & Scott, Greek-English Lexicon, 1843, under "eleemosyna."

derived the German word "Almosen" and the English word "alms." This term "eleemosyna" might imply that the giver bestows a sum in charity upon a needy priest as that same person would throw a dime to a beggar. Because of the theory that Mass stipends constitute a bilateral contract binding in justice rather than in charity, there remains but little use for the word "eleemosyna." The English word "alms" hardly deserves to be mentioned, because it is never used in the same sense as the term "Mass stipend."[2]

The word "honorarium" deserves a little more courtesy. Honorarium means in Latin something that is done in honor of a person; and as a substantive, it signifies an honorary fee or a present. Van Espen[3] applied it to the money given for Masses. In fact, it seems to have been the usual term for this offering long before the name of "stipendium" came into vogue.

Priests frequently use another expression, viz.: intention. A curate will ask his friend, "Father, have you any intentions?" The cynic answers, "Yes, I have plenty of intentions, but no stipends." For the fact remains that the word "intention" is used figuratively and somewhat inaccurately in this connection, because the intention of the donor or of the priest is quite a different thing from the money given to the priest for applying the Mass.

Occasionally, people will say, "I want to pay for a Mass." This expression is not absolutely heretical. Nevertheless, "to pay for a Mass" is an expression that should be discouraged as offensive, ambiguous, mislead-

2 Cf. New Standard Dictionary, Funk & Wagnalls, New York, 1914. Cf. Slater, Cases of Conscience, Vol. II, pp. 135 sqq. Note that this Englishman never uses any other word than stipend. The same is true of Fr. Dolphin, who translated the book called "The Busy Pastor's Guide."

3 Van Espen, Jus Ecclesiasticum, Tom. I, p. 2, tit. 5, c. 5, n. 1, p. 326, no. 35. Cf. Berlandi, Delle Oblazioni, p. 190. "Dum jam sensim Oblatio inter Missarum solemnia pene cessaret, atque in Missis praecipue privatis Oblatio parum nota esset, tunc qui pro se specialiter tanquam Offerente Missam celebrari, et orari volebat, id oblato denario a Secerdote postulabat, atque hine ille denarius, quem hodie Honorarium aut Stipendium vocamus."

ing and bordering on heresy. On the other hand, no sensible priest will reprove a poor woman for giving him "money for Masses"; because he knows that no simony is intended.

Of all the names for this contract, the most common as well as the most accurate one is that of Mass stipends. For centuries priests have been using the words "Missarum stipendia." In English, authors use the term "stipends"; in German the words become a compound, "Mess-stipendien."

The Latin noun, stipendium, is derived from "stips," meaning a small contribution in money, an alms, or a cash present; and the verb pendere, to weigh.[4] Stipendium meant originally a soldier's pay;[5] and St. Jerome[6] used it in this sense.

St. Thomas Aquinas, by his famous distinction, leads one to think that in the thirteenth century the technical meaning of stipend had not yet crystallized; for he adds the differentiating phrase, "ad sustentationem."[7]

No better explanation of the word as it is used by American Catholics can be found than the descriptive definition given in the Catholic Encyclopedia:[8] "By a Mass stipend is meant a certain monetary offering which anyone makes to the priest with the accompanying obligation of celebrating a Mass in accordance with the intentions of the donor (ad intentionem dantis)." Hence, priests ought to cultivate the habit of using the term, Mass stipends; for these words constitute the least objectionable and most precise expression, and they form the technical term whose meaning has been determined by usage and whose use has been sanctioned by the Code.

4 Cf. Freund-Leverett's Lexicon of the Latin Language, word "stipendium."

5 "Stipendium militibus persolvere."

6 I Cor. ix, 7, "Quis militat suis stipendiis unquam?"

7 St. Thomas Aquinas, Summa Theologica, 2-2, q. 100, art. II, ad. 2.

8 Pohle, Cath. Encycl, art. Mass., Vol. X, p. 21.

CHAPTER IV

"PROBATUM"
OR
THE CANONICAL ASPECT OF MASS STIPENDS

An explanation of the three salient words in the first section of the first canon on Mass stipends is in itself a study of Mass stipends in their canonical aspect. But the title affixed to this chapter was chosen because this chapter will contain matter of a more strictly canonical nature.

First of all, attention is called to the fact that in Canon 824 the legislator uses the expression, "morem atque institutum" instead of the usual word "consuetudo." Both Woywod[1] and Augustine[2] disregard this nicety when they call this usage a custom. The Latin word "consuetudo" is a technical term. Vermeersch[3] defines consuetudo as "jus diuturnis populi moribus introductum." Hence a consuetudo or custom is a law; but mores and instituta are not laws.

On the contrary, the Latin word "mos" means a "usage as determined, not by the laws, but by men's will and pleasure."[4] Hence a "consuetudo" is the child of "mores"; and in English, too, one may say that usage gives birth to custom. The substantive "institutum" is translated by practice, ordinance and institution. The Romans united the two nouns, as Americans combine such words as will and testament. Cicero wrote, "quae vero more agentur institutisque civilibus." But the phrase seems to have been taken from the constitution,

1 Woywod, The New Canon Law, p. 166, n. 667.

2 Augustine, A Commentary, Vol. IV, p. 175.

3 Vermeersch-Creusen, Epitome J. C., Vol. I, p. 51, n. 85.

4 Harper's Latin Dictionary, Harper & Bros., New York, 1888. Cf. Crabb, English Synonyms, p. 322 (custom), tenth ed., Harper & Bros., New York, 1858.

"Auctorem fidei," proposition 54, in which are found the identical words, "secundum receptum et probatum Ecclesiae morem et institutum."

Secondly, attention is called to the word "cuilibet" in Canon 824. Apropos of this is the adage, "Ubi lex non distinguit, nec nos distinguere debemus." The Code means what it says when it declares that any priest who applies Holy Mass may accept a Mass stipend. Consequently, a rich priest may accept an alms (sic) in return for a Mass.[5] For every laborer is worthy of his hire; every one, rich or poor, who serves the altar is entitled to his sustenance from the altar; in fine, the accidental wealth of the contracting priest does not change the essential character of the contract to apply a Mass for him who in justice gives him something in return.

Moreover, when two or more priests say Mass together, each may accept the usual Mass stipend.[6] For according to the most common teaching concerning the nature of the Eucharistice Sacrifice, there are as many Masses as there are priests who offer to God His immolated Son. Hence, too, a newly ordained priest may accept a stipend for the application of the very Mass which forms a part of his ordination; and the same thing is true of a bishop as regards the Mass of his consecration.[7] The concelebration of Greek priests will be treated more thoroughly in subsequent pages.

What about the priest who would not say Mass if he had no stipend? Let moralists judge his conduct.

5 Cf. Cappello, De Sacramentis, Vol. I, p. 533, n. 666.

6 Cf. Cappello, De Sacramentis, Vol. I, p. 533, n. 666. He refers to Benedict XIV, De Sacrificio Missae, Lib. III, cap. XVI. Benedict XIV in turn quoted De Lugo, Tractatus De Sacramentis, disput. 19, Sect. 12, n. 252, "si duo Sacerdotes simul consecrarent unam Hostiam, essent duae oblationes, et singuli possent applicare Missam pro diversis."

7 Cf. Cappello, De Sacramentis, Vol. I, p. 534, n. 666. "Quare dubitandum non est quin neo—presbyteri pro Missa ordinationis eleemosynam percipere queant. Idem dicas de neo-episcopo pro Missa consecrationis."

Students of canon law, exonerate such a venal priest from the charge of simony, provided that he does not accept the money as the price or equivalent of the Mass's intrinsic worth. In this manner, canonists explain away the severity of Innocent XI, who condemned the proposition that there is no simony even if the temporal thing be the principal motive for giving the spiritual thing.[8] As far as canon law is concerned, such a priest applies the Mass which he celebrates; and this is all that the Code requires of one who accepts a stipend.

Religious give rise to another problem. Such priests make a vow of obedience. Sometimes their Superior commands them to say Mass for an intention specified by him. Suppose that such a religious priest ignores the precept, accepts a stipend, and applies the Mass "ad intentionem dantis." Such a priest would, of course, be guilty of disobedience and would sin against his vow. Nevertheless, he is the dispenser of the special fruit accruing from his Mass; his intention prevails over that of the Superior; and prescinding from the vow of poverty, he may lawfully keep the Mass stipend.[9]

Jesuits are forbidden, not by canon law, but by their rule, to accept Mass stipends for themselves or for other priests.[10] Consequently, in this matter they are not bound by the canonical restrictions incumbent on other priests. Jesuits are permitted, for example, to accept any sum of money as an alms and to say a few Masses out of gratitude instead of justice. The donor must even understand that he has no strict right to a Mass and that the Jesuit has no strict obligation in justice or even in

8 Innocent XI, prop. 46: Cf. Denzinger, "Enchiridion," n. 1196. "Dare temporale pro spirituali non est simonia . . . etiamsi temporale sit principale motivum dandi spirituale, immo etiamsi sit finis ipsius rei spiritualis, sic ut illud pluris aestimetur quam res spiritualis."

9 Benedict XIV, De Missae Sacrificio, Lib. III, cap. IX, p. 176.

charity to celebrate and apply the Mass for the giver's intention.[10]

Finally, there remain for consideration the Mass stipends which are received by priests who are not in good standing. The Mass produces its essential fruits ex opere operato, and every priest who celebrates and applies a Mass validly may lawfully accept a stipend. Hence, the subject resolves itself into the question, Is there any priest who cannot say Mass validly?

Gratian [11] taught that heretical priests could celebrate Mass validly, but he denied this power in priests who were suspended or deposed. St. Raymond of Pennafort held that excommunicated, heretical and deposed priests could celebrate Mass validly.[12] Innocent III tells us that the Mass of a bad priest is just as truly a Mass as is that of a good priest, because each of them offers sacrifice in the person of the entire Church.[13]

The reason for the stand taken by these canonists is to be found in the indelibility of the sacerdotal character.

10 Cappello, a Jesuit canonist, writes: Sacerdotes Societatis Jesu nec pro se nec pro aliis possunt stipendium Missarum accipere. Institutum enim Societatis prohibet ne pro sacris ministeriis stipendium percipiatur. At titulo eleemosynae potest occasione ministerii aliquid recipi. Hinc si offeratur pecunia pro Missis celebrandis, ea accipi potest tamquam eleemosnya, cum promissione celebrandi ex gratitudine aliquas Missas, dummodo offerens plane intelligat pecuniam non pro Missis accipi, nec ipsum habere jus strictum ad Missam, nec accipientem habere strictam obligationem eas celebrandi." Cappello, De Sacramentis, Vol. I, p. 540, footnote 46. Cf. Benedict XIV, Institutio LVI, n. 1. Cf. Institutum Societatis Jesu, Epitome, p. 185; Cf. Gasparri, De Euch., Vol. I, n. 550.

11 C. 97, C. I. q. I. "Suspenso enim vel deposito sacerdote, nulla ei relinquitur potestas sacrificandi."

12 St. Raymond of Pennafort, Summa (I. I, I, tit. 5, 6, p. 38), "Regulariter teneas, quod episcopi et sacerdotes, sive sint excommunicati, sive haeretici, sive depositi, vera conferunt sacramenta, dum tamen in forma Ecclesiae." Rursusque (1. 3, tit. 24, n. 5, p. 306) "Quantum ad veritatem sacramentorum, non refert a quo (sacerdote) conficiantur, dummodo in forma Ecclesiae conficiantur et conferantur."

13 Innocent III, De Sacro Altaris Mysterio, 1. 3, c. 5, M. P. L. 217, 844. ". . . quia sacerdos non tantum in sua, sed in totius Ecclesiae persona sacrificat. Quapropter in sacramento corporis Christi nihil a bono majus, nihil a malo minus perficitur sacerdote, dummodo sacerdos cum caeteris in arca consistat, et formam observet traditam a columba." Cf. c. 9, col. 848: "Extra unitatem Ecclesiae non est locus offerendi sacrificum unitatis."

The Spouse of Christ may scrape the sacred oils from the hands of a degraded priest; but she cannot erase from his soul the indelible stamp of his priesthood. The Church is really one of the three who offer the Mass of an excommunicated priest, even though she would prefer not to share in his sacrilegious sacrifice. The Church is willing "simpliciter" to have every priest say Mass; but she is unwilling "secundum quid" that an unworthy priest say Mass.[14]

To summarize, every priest rightly ordained, having the proper intention and using the prescribed form, consecrates validly, truly celebrates Mass and efficaciously applies all the special fruit which God attaches to the Mass as such. Since this is so, every priest, even though he be incontinent, simoniacal, disobedient, schismatic, heretical, suspended, degraded or excommunicated; every priest is permitted to keep the stipend accepted for the Mass which he celebrates.

14 De La Taille, Mysterium Fidei, p. 427, text and footnote.

EXPOSITIO TEXTUS

CHAPTER V

BINATION AND TRINATION
OR
CANON 824 / 2

The second section of Canon 824 curtails the permission given in the first section. This second section reads thus: [1]

"Quoties autem pluries in die celebrat, si unam Missam ex titulo justitiae applicet, sacerdos, praeterquam in die Nativitatis Domini, pro alia eleemosynam recipere nequit, excepta aliqua retributione ex titulo extrinseco."

Woywod gives the substance of this sentence in the following words: [2]

"Whenever he (the celebrant) says Holy Mass several times a day and has to apply one Mass from a title of justice, he cannot receive another stipend, excepting some compensation from an extrinsic title. On Christmas, however, he may receive a stipend also for the second and third Mass."

It is hardly necessary to say that a binating priest may accept a stipend for *either* Mass, *e. g.*, he may say the first Mass for his parents and accept a large stipend for the second (High) Mass.

In the dissertation, the subject of bination will be treated only insofar as it bears upon the acceptance of Mass stipends. For the rest, suffice it to say that a priest may lawfully celebrate two or three Masses a day either by privilege or because of necessity. Concerning the privilege, more anon. Anent the necessity, note that this necessity need not be an absolute but only a moral one.

1 Codex Juris Canonici, canon 824,—2.

2 Woywod, The New Canon Law, p. 166, n. 667.

This moral necessity, however, does not mean the personal necessity or indigence of the priest. Benedict XIV said,[3] "Nec valet ratio paupertatis sacerdotum; abusus enim esset intolerabilis facultas alicui sacerdoti facta iterandi Missam eum in finem, ut duplici eleemosyna decentius se sustentaret."

When the daily private Mass became universal about the sixth century, priests soon began to celebrate Mass two, three or more times a day, according to their own caprice.[4] Thus, a century later, Blessed Alcuin celebrated many Masses in one day.[5] From the seventh to the tenth century, the Church silently watched her priests celebrate an ever increasing number of daily Masses. Some of these priests, no doubt, were impelled to this manifold celebration by devotion towards the Blessed Eucharist or by pastoral care for their flock. But many others were urged on by the sole motive of acquiring stipends.[6] In the eleventh century, the first restriction in this regard was imposed upon priests. In the year 1022, the Fifth Canon promulgated in the Council of Seligenstadt forbade priests to celebrate more than three Masses a day.[7]

In the year 1060, Pope Alexander II reluctantly permitted priests to say two Masses, one of the day and one for the poor souls; and he is the author of the oft repeated but non-juridical principle,[8] "Sufficit sacerdoti Missam unam in die celebrare, quia Christus semel passus est." Pope Innocent III (d. 1216) with characteristic energy broke up the abuse of celebrating several Masses on the same day. He repeated the words of Alexander II, but he mentioned the famous exception concerning Christmas. "Consuluisti nos utrum presbyter duas Missas in eodem die valeat celebrare; super quo Respondemus, quod, excepto die Nativitatis dominicae, nisi causa necessitatis

3 Declarasti Nobis, Collectanea, n. 1352—8. Cf. Acta et Decreta Conc. Plen. Amer. Latinae, Rome 1899, Vol. I, p. 163, n. 348.

4 Cf. Cath. Encyclopedia, art. Bination, Vol. II, p. 568.

5 Cf. Migne, P. L., Tome C, p. 104.

6 Cf. Benedict XIV, De Missae Sacrificio, Lib. III, cap. 2.

7 Cf. Hergenröther, Kirchenlexikon, art. Bination, Vol. II, p. 841.

8 c. 53, D. 1, de consecratione.

suadeat, sufficit sacerdoti semel in die unam Missam solummodo celebrare." [9]

His successor, Pope Honorius III, appended to that statement the reason, "nam et felix valde est, qui celebrat digne unam;" and he extended the law to all members of the hierarchy. "Quam cuilibet sacerdoti, quacumque dignitate praefulgeat, unam in die celebrare missam sufficit." [10]

Benedict XIV calls attention to the fact that the question read "valeat celebrare," and the answer, "sufficit celebrare." From these words he concludes that both "sufficit" and "non valeat" mean "non licet." [11]

This Prince of Canonists gives avarice as the main reason why priests were wont to celebrate several Masses on the same day, and he relates that St. Francis of Assissi strove to counteract this tendency by permitting the members of the Franciscan Order to have only one daily Mass.[12]

In the Oriental Church it was always the rule that a priest might celebrate Mass once only each day.[13] The Latin Church forbade her ministers to accept more than one stipend a day before she forbade them to celebrate more than one Mass a day. The reason for the prohibition of a second stipend in case of bination or trination must be sought in the Church's desire to shield her central act of worship from the very appearance of venality. "Ratio constantis inhibitionis recipiendi eleemosynam pro secunda Missa, in hoc posita est, ut omnis avaritia omnisque etiam mercimonii suspicio, a rebus sacris arceatur." "Intentio principalis disponentis (quam semper in applicatione legis attendere oportet) est ut prospiciatur potius disciplinae ecclesiasticae robori, quam sacerdotum utilitati." [14]

9 c. 3, X, de celebratione Missae, III, 41.

10 Cf. C. 12, X, de celebratione, III, 41.

11 Bullarii Romani Continuatio, Vol. II, p. 28.

12 Institutiones Eccl., LVI, n. 2.

13 Cf. Hergenröther, Kirchenlexikon; Vol. II, col. 841, art. Bination.

14 Acta Sanctae Sedis, Vol. XI, pp. 284 and 634.

Not every Mass whose fruit is applied ex justitia has a stipend annexed to itself. For instance: a priest may bind himself not only by the (venial) obligation of fidelity but also by the (serious) obligation of justice to say a Mass for the intention of some other person to whom he has thus promised the Mass. A priest who fulfills such a promise with one Mass may not accept a stipend for another Mass which he happens to celebrate on the same day.

More practical than this promised Mass is the Missa Pro Populo, which every pastor is bound to say for his parishioners on Sundays and holy-days.[18] Since the Code, if not before it, the bishops and rectors in the United States are bound ex justitia and under penalty of mortal sin to apply the Missa Pro Populo.[19] Concerning the Missa Pro Populo, the Sacred Congregation of the Council instructed a certain bishop to warn the pastors in his diocese that they must apply the Mass for their people on the prescribed days, and that they may not accept a stipend for such Masses under any pretext whatsoever.[20]

Hence, the rector of any parochial or even national Church[21] commits a grave sin of injustice towards the people confided to his pastoral care if he fails even once to say the Missa Pro Populo. If he accepts stipends for both Masses on a Sunday, he is bound, not to restore the stipends, but to say the Missa Pro Populo as soon as possible.[22] The same priest would be guilty of serious disobedience if he should accept a stipend for one Sunday Mass and then apply the other Mass for his people, but in this case, he would not be obliged to make any restitution to the parish or to the giver of the stipend, since both have received all that they can justly claim.

18 Cf. canones, 466, 306, 339, etc.

19 S. C. C., July 13, 1918. Cf. Acta Apostolicae Sedis, Vol. XI, p. 46 sqq.; Vol. XI, p. 346, sqq. Cf. Augustine, A. Commentary, Vol. IV, p. 177.

20 S. C. C. Ep. Cameracensi, Sept. 25, 1858; Cf. Acta Sanctae Sedis, Vol. IX, p. 299.

21 A. A. S., XVI, p. 113.

22 S. C. de Prop. Fide, March 11, 1843; Collectanea, n. 964.

Would such a priest or any other priest be allowed to keep the Mass stipends which he has sinfully accepted in violation of Canon 824 / 2? The theoretical answer hinges upon the nature of Mass stipends. Casuists, who deny that a binating priest may keep the stipends given him for both Masses, argue that such a celebrant has no title whatever to the second stipend, because the only title which any priest has to a stipend is the one conferred on him by the Church, and this title is explicitly withheld by Canon 824 / 2.

But the force of this argument is rendered nugatory by the common teaching concerning the contractual nature of Mass stipends. The Code evidently accepts this theory in Canon 826 / 3 and Canon 1544 / 2.[23] Consequently the priest gets his right to the money, not by obeying the law of the Church, but by fulfilling his part of the bilateral agreement. Moreover, Gasparri [25] and Vermeersch [26] teach that a priest is not bound to restore a stipend which he has accepted in violation of Canon 824 / 2. Their authority alone would render this opinion theoretically probable, and therefore, practically certain. But the all important reason is the absence of any canon to the contrary. In practice, therefore, a curate who accepts Mass stipends for both Masses, or a pastor who accepts a stipend for either of his Sunday Masses, may keep the stipends.[27]

Vermeersch and others teach that for a grave reason (*e. g.*, to say a funeral Mass, a nuptial Mass, an anniversary Mass, a Mass for a stipendium pingue), a pastor may apply the Mass for the intention of the giver on Sundays or suppressed holy-days, and postpone the Missa Pro Populo to another day. Or the pastor may say the "five-dollar Mass" and compel his curate to say the Missa

23 "Alia stipendia quae ex fundationum reditibus percipiuntur, appellantur fundata seu Missae fundatae." "Fundatio, legitime acceptata, naturam induit contractus synallagmatici: do ut facias."

25 Gasparri, "De Eucharistia," Vol. I, p. 396, n. 546.

26 Vermeersch, Epitome J. C., Vol. II, p. 7, n. 13.

27 Amer. Eccl. Review, 1924, Vol. LXX, p. 201 ad finem.

Pro Populo for the diocesan stipend (Vermeersch Epitome J. C., Vol. II, n. 108).

A visitor, on the other hand, who celebrates two Masses on Sunday as a favor to the pastor is forbidden to take a stipend for either Mass if he applies the other as the Missa Pro Populo; but the pastor may accept a stipend on that Sunday, because he has transferred to the visitor the obligation of applying the Missa Pro Populo ex justitia.[28] A bishop who accidentally (not regularly) supplies the place of a parish priest would satisfy the obligation of saying the parochial Missa Pro Populo by offering it for the faithful of the entire diocese.

Such a bishop could say the second Mass on that Sunday for some friends of his at whose marriage he had officiated on Saturday afternoon. Conversely, a bishop or priest who assists at a marriage without getting a Mass stipend may say the Missa or the Oratio Pro Sponsis, if the rubrics permit, and still offer the special fruit of the Sacrifice according to his own special intention. The reason is, that the rite of the Holy Sacrifice (Missa Pro Sponsis) is to be distinguished from the fruits of that Sacrifice.[29]

Finally, a priest who binates may licitly fulfill with the one Mass any obligation of justice (titulo justitiae ratione parochiatus, ratione stipendii, ratione beneficii, ratione promissionis de justitia); and with the other Mass fulfill any obligation which does not bind him in justice. Thus a pastor or curate may offer his second Mass on Sunday for the deceased members of the Purgatorial Society (titulo caritatis), or for his own parents (titulo pietatis), or for his benefactors (titulo gratitudinis), or for persons whom he has promised a Mass gratuitously (titulo promissionis), or in fulfillment of a vow which he has made (titulo religionis).

And whilst he is fulfilling this vow or this promise by applying the Mass, he is remunerated by the pastor for the extrinsic inconvenience of celebrating this second

28 Link, Mess-Stipendien, p. 337 and 238.

29 Eccl. Review, 1897, Vol. XVI, p. 180.

parochial Mass. This statement is based upon one of the most significant terms in the whole canon, viz.: titulo extrinseco.

The word "title" means that the applicant of the Mass has a right to the usual recompense, that he may even demand this remuneration, and that the faithful are bound in justice to give him the legal stipend.[30]

The amount of money usually given as a Mass stipend would never constitute absolutely grave matter in itself. But it might readily and frequently constitute relatively grave matter. For there are some "Mass priests," even in this country, who depend mostly on their daily stipend for their daily expenses. And surely an American priest who sends an intention to a priest in Africa or Germany without forwarding the stipend, withholds from the celebrant of that Mass a sum which constitutes relatively grave matter.

If the amount promised or given is slight, some authors think that even then the obligation of giving it is grave. The contradictory opinion, however, seems to be the more probable one; for in this case the giver of the Mass stipend obliges himself to give a trifle, an obligation the violation of which should hardly be deemed a mortal sin.

If the offering is so small that the priest promises a Mass out of charity, rather than confers a right to it from a title of justice, then he certainly is bound only "sub levi" by his promise, unless he expressly intended to bind himself ex justitia et sub gravi.[31] Is it legitimate to infer from this that a priest may accept twenty-five cents as an alms for his first Mass and a dollar stipend for his second Mass on Sundays? No; for Canon 828 states explicitly, "Tot celebrandae et applicandae sunt Missae, quot stipendia etiam exigua data et accepta fuerint."

The extrinsic title to which the Code refers is one which confers on a priest a right to some recompense

30 Cappello, De Sacramentis, Vol. I, n. 668.

31 Cappello, De Sacramentis, Vol. I, n. 668.

for saying Mass without obliging him to apply the fruits of the Mass according to the intention of the person who gives the stipend. In other words, an extrinsic title is one that prescinds from the application of the Mass. For example, a priest who is going away on his vacation asks a fellow-priest to take his place on the following Sunday. Evidently the one who makes the request does not care for whom his substitute offers the Holy Sacrifice, as long as he actually celebrates Mass in the specified Church and at the time prescribed. Now, that substitute has a right to some remuneration, not alone for *saying* Mass, but for saying it at that particular time and place. Very often such a priest must put himself to considerable expense and great inconvenience to accommodate his fellow-priest. One author, at least, goes so far as to intimate that bination itself, apart from all consideration of time, place, expense or accidental inconvenience, always confers upon the celebrant an extrinsic title to remuneration, because of the intrinsic inconvenience which bination invariably entails.[32] His opinion is well founded.[33]

It seems that the Church never permits her priests to accept for their own use stipends for two Masses which are said on the same day. But the Congregation of the Council on August 7, 1909, permitted the clergy of Breda for the next seven years to accept a stipend for the second Mass, and apply the Mass according to the intention of the bishop to whom the stipend was to be handed over. The bishop himself was obliged to use this money for pious purposes. In these pious purposes, the support of poor priests was included; and so, if the celebrant was poor, the bishop was permitted to refund the stipend in whole or in part to him. A similar indult was granted to a French bishop.[34]

The Code confers on every priest of the Latin rite

32 Link, Mess-Stipendien, p. 336.

33 Acta Sanctae Sedis, Vol. XIII, p. 341.

34 S. C. C. Aug. 7, 1909; Cf. Acta Apostolicae Sedis, Oct. 15, 1909. Cf. S. C. C., Feb. 27, 1905, Acta Sanctae Sedis, XXXVII, p. 524.

the privilege of saying three Masses on Christmas and accepting a stipend for each, unless some other obligation precludes such an acceptance. But "the Occidental custom of trinating on Christmas never found its way into the Oriental Church." [35]

Three Masses used to be celebrated by bishops on Holy Thursday, and by priests, too, on Easter, All Souls' Day and the feast of the Baptist's Nativity.[36] St. Ildephonse, a Spanish bishop who flourished in the year 845, alludes to trination on Christmas, Easter, Pentecost and the feast of the Transfiguration.[37]

Trination on Christmas seems to be of almost apostolic origin. For Pope Telesphorus I, who reigned as early as 140 A. D., enacted that on the feast of the Nativity one Mass be celebrated at midnight, a second at the aurora or dawn, and the third after sunrise.[38] Others claim that Christmas itself was introduced into Rome under Pope Liberius, who reigned two centuries after Pope Telesphore, viz.: in 354 A. D. Pope St. Gregory the Great could not preach a long sermon on Christmas, because he was going to celebrate Mass three times that day.[39] Pope Innocent III (died 1216) mentioned Christmas as an exception to the rule that a priest should celebrate Mass once only each day. "Respondemus quod excepto die Nativitatis Dominicae . . . sufficit sacerdoti semel in die unam Missam solummodo celebrare." [40] The reader will notice that the Code appropriates, with slight modification, the phraseology of Innocent III when it refers to Christmas.

Benedict XIV tells that trination was universal in the Western Church. "Pervetustus est, atque universim in Latinam Ecclesiam receptus Ritus trini Sacrificii per

35 Motry, Diocesan Faculties, P. 65.

36 Catholic Encyclopedia, Vol. II, p. 568, art Bination.

37 Migne, P. L., Tom. CVI, col. 888.

38 Amer. Eccl. Review, Vol. XX, p. 212. Vid. Bollandista index, Jan. 5.

39 Greg. Homilia 8 in Evangelium Nativitatis, Migne, Vol. LXXVI, col. 1103.

40 Cf. C. 3, X, de cel. Miss., III, 41.

unumquemque Sacerdotem Natalitio Christi die offerendi; verum apud Orientalem Ecclesiam nullum exstat praefati Ritus vestigium."[41]

The same pope mentions not only the permission of trinating, but of accepting three stipends as well on that exceptional day. "Ubique esse receptum . . . ut in solemnitate Nativitatis Domini pro tribus Missis tria recipiantar charitatis stipendia."[42]

Nothing more need be said about Christmas. But much more remains to be said about trination on All Souls' Day. Ever since the sixth century the priests of Aragon Valencia and Catalaunia had been receiving stipends for all the Masses which they celebrated on All Souls' Day.[43] The Congregation of the Council under Paul V (November 15, 1605), and again under Urban VIII (June 21, 1625), condemned this practice as dangerous and scandalous. When certain eminent men asked these popes to tolerate it in other regions, the Congregation of the Council "petentes urbane dimisit."[44]

Later, Ferdinand VI, King of Spain, asked the Sovereign Pontiff to extend the privilege which obtained in Aragon, to the rest of the Spanish Kingdom and its possessions; and John V, King of Portugal, asked that the same privilege be extended to his kingdom and colonies.[45] In reply, Benedict XIV sent the indult entitled "Quod expensis" and dated August 26, 1748.[46] In that indult the pope urged the priests of Aragon, etc., who already enjoyed the privilege of trination on All Souls' Day, to apply the special fruit of their second and third Masses to all the faithful departed. By the same indult, he gave the privilege of celebrating a third Mass in the Spanish Kingdom, and a second as well as a third Mass in the other regions of Spain and Portugal. Thirdly, he commanded the priests who availed them-

41 Bullarii Romani Continuatio, Vol. III, par. 2, p. 297, sect. 2.
42 Bullarium Romanum, T. XLVII, p. 276.
43 Benedict XIV, De Missae Sac. Lib. III, cap. IV, n. 10.
44 Fontes II, n. 365.
45 Ferreres, "Las Misas Manuales, pp. 30-40.
46 Fontes, II, n. 391.

selves of this privilege by indult, to apply the "fructus medius" of the second and third Masses to all the faithful departed in general, and he strictly forbade that it be applied to any soul in particular. One reason for this law is the fact that many Masses for which stipends have been accepted are never celebrated, because of "reduction" by the Holy See, or because of priests' carelessness, forgetfulness, or because of misfortunes (*e. g.*, because letters containing stipends were stolen or went astray). Another reason might be the fact that the Church, like a benign mother, wishes to help the most abandoned souls in Purgatory, the souls of her children who have no one else on earth to take pity on them.

Benedict XIV did not know, but was ready to believe, that the secular priests of Aragon were permitted by custom to accept two stipends; and "regular" priests three stipends on the feast of All Souls. Concerning these priests, there was to be no innovation. But the other priests, who made use of this indult, were forbidden (sub poena suspensionis a divinis latae sententiae et Ordinario reservata) to accept a stipend for the second or the third Mass.

The historical importance of the document and its strong, clear wording warrant a lengthy quotation from this indult. The text reads thus: [47]

"Sub iisdem poenis praecipimus atque jubemus, ut nonnisi unam accipiant eleemosynam, videlicet pro prima Missa dumtaxat, et in ea tantum quantitate, quae a Synodalibus, Constitutionibus, seu a loci consuetudine regulariter praefinita fuerit. Decernentes nullam omnino causam, nullumque praetextum, aut obtentum, ad declinandam hujus praecepti nostri observantiam suffragari posse, ne voluntariam quidem Fidelium oblationem, nam nec a sponte dantibus quidquam recipi posse statuimus; nec alium quemcumque colorem, quod nempe eleemosyna detur pro celebratione, non autem pro applicatione Missae; aut quod applicatio facienda sit pro

47 Bullarii Romani Continuatio, Vol. II, p. 423; Fontes, Vol. II, n. 391, par. 6.

omnibus Fidelibus Defunctis sive quod offerentes cupiant ipso dumtaxat oblationis merito Defunctos juvare; hi enim poterunt per alia pia opera, sive per alias eleemosynas in alios quoscumque, quam in Sacerdotem, eique conjunctos, erogandas, Defunctorum Animabus, suffragari. Non item gravem indigentiam, aut paupertatem Sacerdotis celebrantis, aut ecclesiae, aut Coenobii; quibus nimirum aliis quibuscumque rationibus subveniendum erit: Nec magnam copiam eleemosynarum, quae congestae fuerint pro Missis celebrandis ipsa die Commemorationis omnium Fidélum Defunctorum, quibusque aliter satisfieri non possit; . . . In summa volumus et statuimus, hujusmodi Missis de novo concessas omnibus in communi Fidelium Defunctorum animabus, absque ulla prorsus eleemosynae perceptione applicari; contrafacientes autem poenam suspensionis a Divinis ipso facto incurrere decernimus."

American canonists, however, were most interested in the sentence:[48] "Hujusmodi consuetudinem, sive ritum, auctoritate nostra extendimus ad alia Regna, et Dominia eidem Hispaniarum Regi subjecta, atque insuper ad ea, quae alteri quidem principi, nimirum Lustianiae Regi parent." For at the time when this privilege was granted the Spanish possessions (Dominia eidem Hispaniarum Regi subjecta) stretched from the Mississippi River westward to the Pacific Ocean and northward to the present State of Oregon, and eastward from the Mississippi River to the Atlantic Coast, and northward up into the Carolinas. And by the Treaty of Paris in February, 1763 (*i. e.*, fifteen years after the granting of this indult), Spain ceded to Great Britain the Province of Florida and all the country to the east and southeast of the Mississippi.[49] Hence, priests in many parts of the United States, except the original thirteen Colonies, have had for almost two centuries the privilege of celebrating three Masses on All Souls' Day.

A provincial Council of Cincinnati proscribed pious

48 Fontes, n. 391.

49 Catholic Encyclopedia, art. Louisiana, Vol. IX, p. 380.

lists by decreeing that as many Masses must be celebrated as the total sum contributed on All Souls' Day constitutes legal diocesan stipends.[50] "Ubicumque die commemorationis Omnium Fidelium aut alia qualibet occasione adhibitis sic dictis 'pious lists' aut alio quocumque medio pecunia confertur a fidelibus intuitu Sacrificii Missae ad intentionem contribuentium applicando, tot semper Missae celebrari debent quot stipendia juxta taxam diocesanam continentur in summa totali sic contributa."

On May 13, 1876, and January 27, 1877, the congregatio de Propaganda Fide, having consulted the Holy Office, tolerated what it assumed to be an existing general custom in the United States.[51] To the bishop who submitted the question, it replied that no innovation was to be made; and to its answer were appended these two explanatory statements:

(I)—Canon law admits of no custom by which the offerings made for several Masses can be legitimately satisfied for by the celebration of one Mass, if anyone makes his offering with the understanding that he will receive as many Masses as his stipend ordinarily represents;

(II)—But where there is no deception or circumvention, or misunderstanding on the part of those who make the offering, a *priest* may accept as a gift of generosity whatever the faithful offer on this occasion.

In extenuation of this practice, let it be said that these pious lists are a source of big income for the poorly remunerated priests of the West; that people do not consider the offerings a formal stipend; and thus waive the rights conferred by Canons 824, 844; that in some places the diocesan statutes regulate this matter, and legislate "Praeter legem" by adding six Masses to the Mass prescribed by the Holy See.[52]

Finally, the very canon under consideration (824 / 2)

50 Decreta Prov. Conc. Cincinnati V.

51 Acta Sanctae Sedis, Vol. X, p. 129.

52 Amer. Eccl. Review, Vol. LXIX, p. 424.

permits a priest to accept titulo extrinseco some remuneration for celebrating a second or third Mass.[53]

The Code confers on priests the privilege of celebrating three Masses on Christmas and on All Souls' Day the privilege of accepting a Mass stipend for every Mass on Christmas, unless they be prevented by some other obligation of justice, and the privilege of accepting titulo extrinseco some remuneration for celebrating a second or third Mass on All Souls' Day.[54]

On December 20, 1879, the Sacred Congregation of the Council granted to the Archbishop of Mexico the faculty of permitting certain priests in his diocese to celebrate three Masses on all Sundays and holy-days of obligation. In virtue of the same rescript, these priests were allowed to keep for themselves the collections which were taken up at the second and the third Masses. The language of the official report of this rescript deserves a moment's attention.[55]

The concession reads, "Posse permitti prudenti arbitrio Episcopi aliquam remunerationem, intuitu laboris et incommodi, exclusa qualibit eleemosyna pro applicatione Missae." This concession was renewed for another term of five years on March 28, 1896; and it furnished a precedent for the exception mentioned in Canon 824 / 2. The report of this rescript appends to the reply the explanation, "Ex quibus colliges . . . Rite indultum fuisse ut plura litari possint sacra et oblatas eleemosynas recipi, uti pretium laboris." [56] What is the meaning of the words "eleemosynas" and "pretium," as well as the signification of the terms "oblatas eleemosynas" and "Pretium laboris"? Whatever their meaning may be, they furnish no convincing argument concerning the relative propriety of the terms applied to Mass stipends; for they refer to an extrinsic, and not to an intrinsic title.

53 A. A. S., XVI, p. 116 for response which proves that canon 824 abrogates decr. S. C. C., 15, Oct., 1915.

54 A. A. S., XVI, p. 116.

55 A. S. S., XIII, pp. 340-344.

56 Acta Sanctae Sedis, Vol. XIII, p. 344.

CHAPTER VI

Illicit Stipends or Canon 825

Whilst Canon 824, the first on the subject, declares Mass stipends in general to be lawful, the next canon mentions four classes of offerings which are illicit. The text of Canon 825 reads thus: [1]

"Nunquam licet:

1°. "Missam applicare ad intentionem illius qui applicationem, oblata eleemosyna, petiturus est, sed nondum petiit et eleemosynam postea datam retinere pro Missa antea applicata;

2°. "Eleemosynam recipere pro Missa quae alio titulo debetur et applicatur;

3°. "Duplicem eleemosynam pro eiusdem Missae applicatione accipere;

4°. "Alteram recipere eleemosynam pro sola celebratione, alteram pro applicatione eiusdem Missae, nisi certo constet unam stipem oblatam esse pro celebratione sine applicatione."

This law is translated as follows: [2]

"It is never lawful:

1. "To apply Holy Mass for the intention of one who may offer a stipend in the future, but who has not yet asked for the Mass, and then to accept the stipend afterwards given for the Mass said before;

2. "To accept a stipend for a Mass that was due and applied from another title;

1 Cf. Codex Iuris Canonici, canon 825.

2 Cf. Woywod, The New Canon Law, p. 167, n. 668.

3. "To receive two stipends for the application of one Mass;

4. "To receive one stipend for only the celebration, and another for the application of one and the same Mass, unless it is certain that one stipend was offered for the celebration without the application."

The word "nunquam" might lead one to think that this canon is an enunciation of the natural law, which admits of no exception or dispensation. History, however, bears witness to the fact that Pope Julius II, Pope Leo X, and the Council of Trent permitted priests to satisfy for two or more stipends with one Mass.[3] Consequently, since the infallible Church cannot sanction by positive law an action forbidden by the natural law, the obvious conclusion is that Canon 825 is simply an eccelesiastical law, a human law from which the pope can dispense.

The word "licet" shows that the law which it introduces is not nullifying but only disciplinary.[4] Nevertheless, the priest who violates it is bound to make restitution, not because the ecclesiastical law has made his contract void, but because he has not fulfilled his part of the contract, as that contract is understood by the people who give the stipends and by the Church's laws which regulate the contract. The manner in which such a priest should make restitution will be explained presently.

The first number or clause of Canon 825 forbids the celebrant of a Mass to apply it for the intention of that person who will give the next stipend or who God foresees will be the next to make an offering. Such a Mass is not applied to anyone in particular because the celebrant has not sufficiently "determined" or specified his intention in the requisite human way; and the special fruit of such an unapplied Mass goes into the spiritual treasury of the Church.[5] Pope Paul V (d. 1621) forbade

3 Cf. p. 65 of this dissertation, chapter VII.

4 Cf. Canon 11.

5 Blat, Comment. Liber III. De Rebus, Pars. I, p. 151, Sed Cf. Gasparri, "De Eucharistia," Vol. I, n. 492.

the practice because of the scandal that it occasioned. For the practice of celebrating a Mass before it has been requested and later accepting an offering for that Mass, deters the faithful from giving stipends, because the people suspect that priest of taking the money without discharging the obligation imposed by its acceptance. Moreover, it prevents the giver of the stipend from attending the Mass or at least from disposing himself more perfectly by contrition, Confession or Communion, to profit by the fruits of that Mass.[6]

As regards stipends, a Mass which is applied before it has been requested must be considered non-existent. Hence, if an offering is made to the celebrant later on, he must say another Mass for the intention of the giver, or refund the money, or consider himself guilty of a grave sin against commutative justice.[7]

The words, "nondum petiit," call for some elucidation. From these words "non dum petiit," it is evident that a wedding may be arranged for, and the Nuptial Mass celebrated, long before the stipend and the stole fee are given to the celebrant of the Mass or the pastor of the parish. Likewise, a widow may tell the priest, "As soon as the insurance is paid to me, I shall bring you the money for saying my husband's Funeral Mass;" and canon law places no barrier in the way of the priest who makes such an agreement, celebrates the Mass and later accepts the money due to him.

This case, however, differs widely from another, which authors discuss at length. A priest, they say, foresees that he will soon be asked to say Mass for a man who has just died; and he reasons that it would benefit the departed soul more to have a Mass said immediately than to wait until the stipend is forthcoming. St. Alphonsus[8] admitted that under such circumstances a priest might apply a Mass and later accept a stipend for

6 Cf. Schmalzgrueber, Jus Ecclesiasticum Universum, Vol. VII, p. 498, n. 128.

7 Blat, Comment. Liber III, pars. I, p. 151 ad finem.

8 Cf. St. Alphonsus, Theol. Mor. 1, 6, n. 337, resp. 125.

it. Vermeersch[9] reconciles this old opinion with the Code's absolute prohibition by teaching that a priest may accept a stipend for a Mass which was said before it was requested, provided that the giver of the stipend ratify the proceeding upon notification. For example, some one tells a priest, "Here are two dollars for two 'Spiritual Bouquets' for John Doe." The priest asks, "May I use the Mass which I said for John Doe this morning as one of these bouquets if I say the Mass for him tomorrow and fill in these cards accordingly?" If the person giving the money say, "Yes," then the priest may accept the one stipend for the Mass which he has already celebrated and applied.

According to the second paragraph of Canon 825, it is never lawful to receive a stipend for a Mass which is due from another title. Blat[10] teaches that the title referred to is any obligation which binds in conscience, even though it does not bind ex justitia. Vermeersch, however, interprets the word "title" somewhat differently. He says,[11] "Non licet . . . stipendium recipere pro Missa quae iam *ex justitia* et titulo oneroso debetur vel quae utcumque ad alteram primam intentionem applicatur."

It would seem that by following this probable opinion, Father James might say one Mass for Father John, thereby discharge his obligation ex caritate of saying a Mass for this deceased member of the Purgatorial Society, and at the same time accept a stipend from Father John's mother for that Mass. Pastors, however, and all others who are obliged to apply the Missa Pro Populo from a title of justice (titulo officii seu ratione muneris), are forbidden by Canon 825, n. 2, to accept a stipend for such a Mass.[12]

9 Cf. Vermeersch, Epitome I, C., Vol. II, p. 52, n. 105 ad 3. ". . . nisi oblator monitus rem ratam habeat."

10 Cf. Blat, Comment, Liber III, Pars. I, p. 152.

11 Cf. Vermeersch, Epitome I, C., Vol. II, p. 52, par. 105, n. 2.

12 Cf. Benedictus XIV, ep. encycl. "Cum semper oblatas," 19 Aug., 1744—2; Fontes, Vol. I, p. 825. "Nec. . . . eleemosynam. . . . percipere posse." Cf. Innocentius XII, const. "Nuper a congregatione," 24 April 1699; Fontes, Vol. I, n. 262.

The third paragraph of the canon under consideration forbids priests to accept two stipends for the application of the same Mass. On September 24, 1665, Pope Alexander VII condemned the following propositions:[13]

"Duplicatium stipendium potest sacerdos pro eadem Missa licite accipere, applicando petenti partem etiam specialissiman fructus ipsimet celebranti correspondentem, idque post decretum Urbani VIII.

"Non est contra justitiam pro pluribus Sacrificiis stipendium accipere, et sacrificium unum offerre. Neque etiam est contra fidelitatem etiamsi promittam promissione, etiam juramento firmata, danti stipendium, quod pro nullo alio offeram."

The acceptance of two stipends for the same Mass may be traced back to the "Missa Bifaciata" explained on page 17 of this dissertation. The priests who resorted to this practice soothed their consciences with the drug of specious sophistry. Relying on the theory that the Mass's fruit which is applied to one person does not benefit him more than the fruit which is applied to several persons, these priests argued that no fraud is committed by the celebrant who accepts a two-fold offering for the same Mass, and where there is no deception there is no injustice (Scienti et volenti non fit injuria). Most people, however, who give a stipend rightly expect to get the entire special fruit of the Holy Sacrifice, which fruit the Code obliges the celebrant to give them; and so the violation of this canon would beget fraud and injury and need of restitution.[14]

Again, there were those who interpreted the text that he who serves the altar should also live by the altar, to mean that the priest's daily stipend should suffice for his daily support; and they reasoned that he who gives only one-half of the usual offering is entitled to no more than one-half of the Mass's fruits. This argument was refuted by the contention that the Mass stipend should not suffice for the priest's sustenance, because every

13 Cf. Denzinger, Enchiridion, n. 979 & 981 (resp. 1108 & 1110).
14 Cf. Schmalzgrueber, Jus Eccl. Univ., Vol. VII, p. 500, n. 130.

priest in good standing has other sources of income, such as salary, stole fees, etc.[15]

Lastly, they reasoned from analogy that, as an underpaid servant may resort to occult compensation, so a priest who is given an inadequate offering may make up the deficit by accepting another stipend from a second person, to whom he applies a part of the Mass's fruit. This argument is refuted by the principle that as a servant who voluntarily agrees to do something for less than a just remuneration may not resort to occult compensation, so the priest may not accept a second stipend for a Mass without the express consent of both donors.[16]

The last number of Canon 825 says that it is never lawful to accept an offering for the celebration of the Mass and another stipend for the application of the same Mass, unless it is evident that one offering was made for the celebration alone regardless of the application.

In some instances there can be no doubt that the money is given for the celebration alone. Thus priests who "help out" on Sundays are remunerated by the pastor, and they are free to accept a stipend for applying the Mass, unless the pastor expressly tells them to say the Mass for an intention specified by him. Nevertheless, the burden of proof lies upon the celebrant who contends that either of his offerings was given to him for the celebration regardless of the application of his Mass.[17] Circumstances which justify the priest in presuming that the mere celebration of a Mass has been requested are: the convenience of the people, the unmistakable language of the giver, and legitimate custom.[18]

15 Gasparri, De SS. Eucharistia, Vol. I, n. 554, p. 400.

16 Cf. Benedictus XIV, ep. encycl. "Demandatam," 24 Dec. 1743, —10; Fontes, n. 338. ". . . et nisi iidem Offerentes unica Missae celebratione se voti compotes fore diclarent, sciat se unico Sacrificio plurium voluntati minime satisfactorum."

17 Cf. Benedict XIV, De SS. Missae Sacrificio. "Nam pro Sacrificii applicatione obtinenda satis est, ut ipsius Celebratio indicatur."

18 Cf. S. C. C. 19 Nov. 1904 in Acta Sanctae Sedis, Vol. XXXVII, p. 590.

CHAPTER VII

FOUNDED MASSES OR CANON 826

The first canon of the Code's Article on Mass Stipends does not define the subject of which that article treats; but it does enumerate the elements or notes from which a definition of these offerings can be formed and from which a correct concept of these fees can be obtained. The next canon explains the descriptive statement which is made in the preceding canon. The third canon, viz.: Canon 826, divides Mass stipends into three classes and explains each class. The text of Canon 826 reads:

"Stipendia quae a fidelibus pro Missis offeruntur sive ex propria devotione, veluti ad manum; sive ex obligatione etiam perpetua a testatore propriis heredibus facta, manualia dicuntur.

"Ad instar manualium vocantur stipendia Missarum fundatarum, quae applicari non possunt in proprio loco, aut ab iis qui eas applicare deberent secundum tabulas fundationis et ideo de jure aut Sanctae Sedis indulto aliis sacerdotibus tradendae sunt ut iisdem satisfiat.

"Alia stipendia quae ex fundationum reditibus percipiuntur, appellantur fundata seu Missae fundatae."

A translation of this canon reads:[1]

"Manual stipends are called those which the faithful offer out of their own devotion, or from some obligation, even a perpetual one imposed on heirs by the testator.

"Ad instar manualium are called the stipends of foundation Masses which cannot be applied in the proper church, or not by those who, according to the laws of those foundation Masses, should say them, and which may

1 Woywod, The New Canon Law, p. 167, n. 669.

either by law or by papal indult be given to other priests to say.

"Other stipends received from a fund set apart for foundation Masses are called Stipenda fundata, or Missae fundatae."

This cannon is based on the second part of the first number in the decree "Ut Debita," which was issued by the Sacred Congregation of the Council under date of May 11, 1904.[2] That decree is a summary of the old laws on manual stipends, and it forms the basis of the Code's whole title on Mass stipends. That part of the decree which corresponds to Canon 826 / 1 and / 2, may well be quoted here for purposes of comparison.

"Declarat in primis Sacra Congregatio manuales Missas praesenti decreto intelligi et haberi eas omnes quas fideles oblata quomodocumque sive brevi manu, sive in testamentis, hanc stipem tradant, dummodo perpetuam fundationem non constituant, vel talem ac tam diuturnam ut tamquam perpetua haberi debeat.

"Ad instar manualium vero esse, quae in aliqua ecclesia constitutae, vel in propria ecclesia hac illave de causa applicare non possunt, et ideo aut de jure aut cum S. Sedis indulto, aliis sacerdotibus tradi debent ut iisdem satisfiat."

Long before the manual Masses and founded Masses were mentioned in the Decree "Ut Debita," Benedict XIV had explained the synonyms of those terms in his "Institutiones."[3] "Nemo ignorat perpetuas alias, alias vero adventitias Missas nuncupari, Primae quidem quotidie, vel certis quibusdam diebus ratione Beneficii, aut Fundatoris instituto, vel Testatoris voluntate celebrantur; adventitiae vocantur; pro quibus stipendium a Fidelibus traditur, ita tamen ut nullus fundus, nullumque onus in futurum tempus constituatur."

Most of the so-called founded Masses in the United States scarcely constitute real foundations in the canonical sense of the term. And American bishops are

2 Cf. Acta Sanctae Sedis. Vol. XXXVI, p. 672.

3 Cf. Benedict XIV, Inst. LVI, X.

prudently loath to give their consent to a perpetual foundation. For the civil law might not recognize a "reduction" by the Holy See; and so the heirs in the event of such a reduction might easily sue the Church and have the bequest restored to them.

Neither the Code nor the decree "Ut Debita" defines a foundation or a founded Mass, but the clause, "dummodo perpetuam fundationem non constituant," indicates a specific difference between founded stipends and all other Mass stipends. A founded stipend or a founded Mass (for the Code uses the terms synonymously) is derived from the perpetual interest or other income on a legacy. Neither the legacy nor the interest which it bears constitutes the founded Mass stipend: they are only the sources from which the stipend as such is derived.[4]

Second, the capital or fund of a foundation is bequeathed, not to any individual priest, but to the Catholic Church. This is a salient difference between a legacy of manual stipends and a bequest for a founded Mass. For example, James by his will leaves one thousand dollars to Father John for Masses. Father John has the option of saying a thousand Masses or of investing the money and having fifty Masses celebrated annually by himself or others as long as the capital exists. These Masses, however, are not founded Masses, because the money was entrusted to an individual priest instead of to the Catholic Church in the person of the Ordinary of a diocese or the Superior General or Provincial of a religious community, *i. e.*, a moral person.[5]

If the obligation is not perpetual but only temporary (*e. g.*, for the rest of the priest's life), the bequest does not constitute a foundation; and consequently it may be accepted, as far as the Code is concerned, by any priest without the consent of his Ordinary or his religious Superior.[6] On the contrary, if a priest should contract

4 Cf. Vermeersch, Epitome Juris Canonici, Vol. II, n. 104, p. 52.

5 Cf. Canones 198, 368, 531, Decret, Urban VIII, 21 Juni 1625; Link, p. 26.

6 Cf. Link, Mess-Stipendien, p. 262, b.

for a founded Mass, or accept the bequest for a founded Mass, without the express permission of his Ordinary or Provincial, his contract would be grievously sinful.[7]

To avoid all complications arising from the civil law, all bequests (of real estate, testamenta) and legacies (of personal property; legata) for foundations should be made to the Ordinary. He should be empowered to reduce the number of Masses according to the fluctuation of the interest on the capital, and also to have the Masses celebrated in another church if they cannot be said conveniently in the one designated. By the terms of the will itself, the priest's obligation ought to cease whenever the fund is lost or yields no income.

All concerned must bear in mind that "devises for religious and charitable uses are valid and binding in foro conscientiae, even though null according to law." [8] The prudent course for the executor and the heirs to follow, is to relieve themselves of all legal and moral responsibility by a legal transfer of the bequest to the Bishop.[9] Although each Ordinary may establish the minimum amount of money which he will accept for a foundation, as he also prescribes the amount of a manual stipend, still the endowment for every annual Low Mass ought to be at least $50.00 and for every High Mass $100.00.[10]

Thirdly, if the perpetual celebration, but not the application, of a Mass is prescribed by the founder, this foundation might constitute a benefice (lay or ecclesiastical), but it would not constitute a founded Mass.[11] For example, a wealthy person might leave enough money to build a Church in his native village and to pay the

7 Cf. Smith, Elements of Eccl. Law, Vol. I, p. 595.

8 Cf. Smith, Elements of Eccl. Law, Vol. I, n. 588, p. 321.

9 Cf. Dillon, Bequests for Masses, Chicago, p. 56—"If it be desired to create a perpetual annuity (i. e., a Missa fundata), frame the bequest so that two distinct grounds may be relied on for holding it to be a good charitable trust, viz: (a) that it is for the support of a minister of religion as such; and (b) that it is for the performance of an act of public worship."

10 Ibid, n. 596. Cf. Conc. Pl. Balt. II, n. 379. Cf. Smith, l. c., n. 596.

11 Cf. Monasterien, S. C. Rituum, Juni 11, 1845, rel. in Cameracen.

salary of the priest who says Mass there daily for the convenience of the village folk. Such benefices are numerous in Italy and Germany, but comparatively rare in America.[12]

Concerning the celebration of founded Masses, the founder or his heirs may designate the celebrant and also prescribe the number, church, altar, day and hour of those Masses. Although the Ordinary is the canonical executor of all bequests to pious causes, still he has no right to interfere as long as the legal executor carries out the provisions of the will.[13] If the beneficiaries by a will are given the choice between a founded Mass and an equivalent number of manual Masses, the manual Mass is to be preferred.[14]

Finally, the bequest must call for the application of the Mass according to the intention of the founder. Expressions like orare, celebrare, cantare, Missas legere, require the application as well as the celebration of the Masses.[15] A non-sectarian society (*e. g.*, the Elks) cannot establish a founded Mass for its deceased members.[16] Unless the contrary is stated explicitly, the bequest is presumed to call for the application as well as the celebration of the Mass; and so no other Mass stipend may be accepted by the beneficiary.[17] Likewise, the celebrant of the conventual Masses, which cathedral and collegiate chapters are bound to offer for their benefactors, is not allowed to take a stipend for those Masses.[18]

In theory, the Catholic Church, which will exist till the end of time, can accept and fulfill a perpetual contract such as a foundation of Masses involves; in practice, the Church has done all that was humanly possible

12 S. C. C. 12 Nov. 1727; Link, p. 273.

13 Cf. Smith, Elements of Eccl. Law, Vol. I, n. 588, p. 321.

14 Link, Mess-Stipendien, p. 265, n. 3.

15 Cf. S. C. C. 13 Apr. 1726; 15 Dec. 1731; 22 Mar. 1766; 28 Apr. 1629; apud Link, Mess-Stipendien, p. 264.

16 Cf. Münstersches Pastoralblat, Vol. XXI, p. 127. Cf. Link, p. 270.

17 Cf. S. C. C. 12 Juli, 1760. Link, Mess-Stipendien, p. 272.

18 Cf. Ballerini-Palmieri, Opus Theol. Mor., Vol. IV, n. 244, p. 737.

for her to do in keeping her part of these contracts.[19] But war, fire, earthquakes, deterioration in the value of money or other bequests, the secularization monasteries, the malice of enemies, all these combined have made it impossible for the Church to celebrate some of the countless Masses to which she has bound herself by the fetters of an eternal contract.

Julius II and Leo X, considering these human contingencies and the superhuman power of loosing committed to themselves as popes, granted to the Order called the Minims, the favor of substituting Collects for Masses. "Collectae, quae dicuntur in eorum Missis, valerent ac si essent Missae integrae ita quod, si dicerent tres aut quatuor Collectas, vel plures, valerent ac si tres; quatuor, vel plures Missas dicerent." [20]

The Council of Trent endowed Bishops and religious Superiors with the faculty, of "Statuere circa haec (legata) quidquid magis ad Dei honorem et cultum atque ecclesiarum utilitatem viderint expedire; ita tamen, ut eorum semper defunctorum commemoratio fiat, qui pro suarum animarum salute legata ea ad pios usus relinquerunt." [21] These pontifical and conciliar concessions come perilously near to sanctioning the Missa Sicca, which has been treated of in previous pages.

The Tridentine faculty conferred on Bishops and religious Superiors the threefold power of condonation, reduction and translation of founded Masses. Each of these three powers demands a paragraph of explanation.

A condonation (condonatio) is an indult by which the Holy See permits a priest to satisfy with one Mass or in another easy way for a number of Masses which should have been celebrated in the past from a title of justice. The Holy Father makes up the deficit out of the inexhaustible spiritual treasury of the Church.[22] Formerly he used to grant condonations in person or

19 Matt., xvi, 16-18.
20 Link, p. 290.
21 Sess. 25, de ref., cap. 4.
22 Cf. Canon 1518.

through the Poenitentiaria, the Congregatio Concilii, the Congregatio Rituum, but most frequently through the Congregatio de Fabrica S. Petri.[23] At the present time, the Congregation of the Council grants reductions of founded Masses because of the depreciation of the fund; condonations for any other reason must be sought from the Congregation of the Sacraments. The Congregation of the Council grants to bishops in the United States and other countries, the faculty, "Reducendi per quinquennium ob diminutionem redituum perpetua Missarum onera," etc.

The sixth faculty of the Apostolic Delegate to the United States empowers him to absolve those who accumulate stipends and spend them with the result that they can hardly say all the Masses which they are bound to celebrate. The guilty priest or his confessor should write to the Apostolic Delegate. If the culprit is not a "recidivus," His Excellency will reduce the series of Masses by instructing the penitent to have a number of Masses celebrated (per se vel per alium) every month. The Apostolic Delegate can reduce the number of manual or founded Masses in the one case only, that the Masses were omitted. For all other reductions, recourse must be had to the Congregation of the Sacraments.

A condonation always refers to the past, whereas a reduction of Masses looks to the future. Reductions are based upon the doctrine that the fruits of a Mass are indefinite and the spiritual treasury of the Church immeasurable, upon the fact that a priest who cannot or will not celebrate a thousand Masses may be able and willing to say a hundred Masses, and on the principle that a reduction makes up in security of application what it takes away in number of celebrations.

The Tridentine faculty and all cognate privileges were revoked by Urban VIII through the Constitution, "Cum saepe contingat" of June 21, 1625.[24] In that Constitution the Sovereign Pontiff reserved the power of re-

23 Link, Mess-Stipendien, p. 292.

24 Cf. C. 1517-2 and Pont. Com. for the Int. of the Code, July 14, 1922.

duction to the Holy See and recognized in bishops only a delegated power of reducing the number of Masses. This reservation imposed upon the Roman authorities the burden of examining and deciding the merits of all petitions for reductions. This burden soon became so unbearable as to necessitate another decentralization of power by means of indults to individual Ordinaries and later through general triennial faculties. These triennial faculties are still granted to any bishop for the asking; but in using these faculties, the Ordinary must be guided by specified principles.

Thus, the bishop or vicar general must bear in mind that, since his power of reduction is a delegated one, his act is null if performed without sufficient cause.[25] However, a canonical reason of great moment is the fact that for decades the founded Mass had been celebrated faithfully for a small stipend. Again, a reduction of Masses may be deemed necessary when the income from the fund is no longer proportionate with the burden imposed. Canonists disagree on the question whether a notable increase in the revenue of a foundation carries with it an obligation of celebrating more Masses; but since this duty is not certain, a priest in practice need not say more Masses than the founder specifies.[26]

Thirdly, the Bishop ought to remove some incidental obligation rather than resort to the extreme measure of reducing the number of Masses; *e. g.*, he should let the priest celebrate Low Masses in lieu of High Masses. A A perpetual reduction should be withheld if a temporary reduction will suffice. A reduction may be granted to a convent which lacks sufficient priests to celebrate all its founded Masses. But after every reduction there no longer remains the duty of making a commemoration of the deceased persons for whom the application was prescribed.[27] Such commemorations used to be made by inserting a Collect in the Mass, or by including the persons'

25 Cf. Canon 84, 1517, 1544, 1551.

26 Cf. Pasquaglio, qu. 1078.

27 Cf. Conc. Trid., sess. 25, de ref., c. 4.

names in the Memento of the Mass, or most frequently by celebrating one or more Masses for the intentions of all the founders. Finally, no Bishop can reduce the same foundation more than once without special delegation: reductio reductionis non valet.[28]

When neither a condonation of past Masses nor a reduction of future Masses nor a combination of the two meets the requirements of a particular foundation: the Ordinary may resort to a third remedy, viz., the translation or permanent transfer of a founded Mass from one place or time to another. Bishops request and obtain the faculty of translation along with the faculties of condonation and reduction. An Ordinary may transfer a founded Mass from one church to another or from one altar to another (translatio loci); or he may change the day or the hour when the Masses are to be said (translatio temporis).

Only for weighty reasons may a Mass be transferred permanently from one time or place to another. Recognized reasons for such a transfer are: the consent of the parties concerned, danger of haphazard celebration in the one church, with greater certitude of celebration in the other church; rejection of the foundation by the priest mentioned in the will of the founder; lack of priests; destruction of the church with no prospect of its being rebuilt; expulsion of religious from the church monastery where the Mass was founded.

Nevertheless, the Ordinary should be slow to exercise his power of translation, remembering that cogent necessity alone justifies a transfer if the founder has shown a predilection for a certain altar or if he founded the Mass for the convenience of the people.[29] If the Bishop or Vicar General does decide to use the faculty of translation, he ought to transfer the founded Mass to the same kind of altar (*e. g.* Blessed Virgin's Altar)

28 Cf. Zamborri, Missa—12, n. 272, 284, 296, 304.
29 Cf. Link, Mess-Stipendien, p. 279.

or to a day of equal rank (*e. g.* Sunday to Sunday, not from feast to ferial).[30]

Then, too, a permanent translation ought to be avoided if a temporary transfer will do.

A quasi-manual stipend (ad instar manualium) is an offering which a priest receives for saying a founded Mass which cannot be celebrated in the place or by the person designated in the foundation. For instance, John leaves a thousand dollars to a seminary with the obligation of a monthly Mass to be said in the seminary for his intention. Realizing that all the professors will be away on their vacation during the summer, the rector of the seminary gives the curate of a neighboring parish five dollars and asks him to say a Mass "ad intentionem dantis" during July. These five dollars would constitute a "stipendium ad instar manualium," or quasi-manual stipend.[31] This would be a case in which the stipend is transferred "de jure," for canon law permits a beneficiary to fulfill his obligation temporarily through a substitute for a grave reason, such as sickness or legitimate absence.[32]

If, however, the benefactor had prescribed that the Mass be celebrated in the Sisters' Chapel at the seminary, then that Mass could not be transferred even for the summer without the Bishop's consent; for such a benefactor is presumed to have endowed the Mass for the convenience of the Sisters.[33]

Whenever the Holy See, by general faculties or particular rescript, permits a translation or permanent transfer of a founded Mass from one church to another, the revenue which the priest receives for the saying of the Mass in the second church constitutes a quasi-manual

30 Cf. S. C. C. 13 Sept. 1782; Cf. Conc. Trid., sess. 25, de ref., n. 7.

31 Cf. S. C. C. 19 Dec. 1904 Acta Sanctae Sedis, Vol. XXXVII, p. 521 sqq. Cf. Hilling, Mass-Stipendien, p. 18.

32 Cf. Decret S. C. C. Ut Debito, 11 Maii, 1904, n. 15; A. S. S., Vol. 36, p. 576. Cf. Ballerini-Palmieri, Opus Theologicum Moral, Prati, 1893, Vol. IV, p. 743, n. 256.

33 Cf. S. C. C. 19 Nov. 1718; 12 Nov. 1727; 11 Jun. 1729; Cf. Link, p. 273.

stipend, which is given "de Sanctae Sedis indulto."[34] For instance, John founds a Mass in St. Joseph's Church. This church is abandoned because all the parishioners have moved away; and the founded Mass is transferred or translated to St. Henry's Church. The pastor who gets the *revenue* from that foundation and says the Masses in St. Henry's Church receives that money as quasi-manual stipends.[35]

34 Cf. Canon 826—2.

35 Cf. S. C. C. 19 Dec. 1904; Acta Sanctae Sedis, Vol. XXXVII, pp. 521. sqq.

CHAPTER VIII

TRAFFIC IN STIPENDS
OR
CANON 827

The canons which explain and classify Mass stipends are followed by a general law against any real or apparent traffic in offerings. Canon 827 reads, "A stipe Missarum quaelibet etiam species negotiationis vel mercaturae omnino arceatur." Woywod translates this,[1] "Any kind of negotiation or trading with Mass stipends must absolutely be avoided." The canon, however, seems to mean rather that "even the appearance of negotiation or trading should be kept away from Mass stipends." This law sounds like an echo from the Council of Trent, which commanded the Bishops to keep the Holy Sacrifice aloof from avaricious irreverence, exactions of alms, and everything else which might stain stipends with the taint of simony or venality.[2]

The Latin noun "mercatura" as used in Canon 827 corresponds in meaning with the English substantive "bartering," implying the exchange of merchandise; whereas the term "negotiatio" refers rather to such business dealings as involve money, checks or bonds.[3] The following examples illustrate four classes of crimes which Canon 827 proscribes:

1. Negotiatio—a man collects two-dollar stipends, engages a priest to say the Masses for one dollar each, and keeps the surplus dollar from each stipend;

2. Species Negotiationis—a man collects stipends for

1 Woywod, "The New Canon Law," n. 670, p. 167.

2 Conc. Trid. sess. XXII, de obserandis et evitandis in celebratione Missae.

3 Cf. Vermeersch, "Epitome Iuris Canonici," Vol. II, p. 53, n. 105, par. 6.

a priest, who agrees to celebrate all the Masses for a dollar each and let the collector keep the surplus;

3. Mercatura—a publisher, instead of sending the money which he has collected as stipends for Masses, sells the celebrants of those Masses a set of books and thereby makes a profit from the books and a commission on the stipends;

4. Species Mercaturae—a publisher gathers stipends, has the Masses said by priests who accept books instead of money from him, but he makes no gain from the stipends as such, except the usual profit on the sale of the books.[3]

But if the object of the exchange is not profit but mutual convenience, a priest may lawfully accept something else instead of money. For instance, he may agree to celebrate a number of Masses which is proportionate to the price of the Mass wine which he is wont to buy from a certain monastery.[a]

The Bishop may even permit the rectors of *poor* churches to demand as payment for wine, candles, laundry, etc., a moderate portion of the stipend received by visiting priests who say Mass there out of devotion, for the sake of convenience, or for any other personal reason.[b]

Then, too, there is a sacerdotal adage, "Ubi Missa, ibi mensa," which means that breakfast should be served to a visiting priest at the rectory of the church where he happens to say Mass. Urbanity, indeed, may entitle this priest to such convenient service; but justice permits the pastor of that church to demand a portion of the Mass stipend in payment for the celebrant's repast.[c]

3 Cf. Vermeersch, "Epitome Iuris Canonici," Vol. II, p. 53, n. 105, par. 6.

a S. C. C., 24 April, 1875; Collectanea, n. 1443.

b Canon 1303, n. 2.

c Gasparri, "De Eucharistia," Vol. I, p. 445, n. 608, "At si celebranti datur collatiuncula, e. g., cafeum, licite potest retineri ex Missae eleemosyna iustum eiusdem pretium, nisi de collatiuncula praebenda, praeter eleemosynam, conventum tacite vel expresse fuerit."

Reference has just been made to four crimes. At first blush, the term might seem to be too strong for those actions, some of which are not even sinful in themselves. But a perusal of Canon 2324 reveals the fact that these four violations of Canon 827 have all the earmarks of ecclesiastical crimes (delicta). For Canon 2324 prescribes penalties like suspension and excommunication as punishments which the Ordinary may inflict upon people who traffic in stipends.[4] It is true that, by making the censures "ferendae sententiae," the Code has mitigated the penalty (viz.: Excommunicatio latae sententiae et Sanctae Sedi simpliciter reservata), which Benedict XIV [5] imposed upon laymen and which Pius IX [6] extended to all profiteering collectors of Mass stipends.[7] Nevertheless, the sanctions which Canon 2324 attaches to Canon 827 prove that persons who traffic in Mass stipends are guilty of canonical crimes.

Another notable abuse against which Canon 827 has been fulminated, consists in imposing stipends as a penance in confession. An antique "Liber Poenitentialis" makes one Mass correspond to twelve days' penance and thirty Masses to a whole year of fasting.[8] In the year 1195, the Council of York forbade confessors to celebrate the Masses which they had imposed upon their penitents; and five years later the Council of London forbade confessors to give Masses as penance to anyone except priests.[9] The Second Plenary Council of Baltimore went even farther by forbidding the acceptance of any stipend in the confessional.[10]

It is also forbidden to demand a higher stipend for

4 Cf. Canon 2324, "Qui deliquerint contra praescriptum Can. 827, 828, 840, n. 1, ab Ordinario pro gravitate culpae puniantur, non exclusa, si res ferat, suspensione aut beneficii vel officii ecclesiastici privatione, vel si de laicis agatur, excommunicatione."

5 Benedict XIV, const. "Quanta Cura," Jan. 30, 1741; Fontes, n. 311.

6 Pius IX, const. "Apostolicae Sedis," Oct. 12, 1869.

7 Leech, "A Comparative Study," p. 67.

8 Geier, "De Missarum Stipendiis, p. 58.

9 Hardouin, "Acta Conciliorum," Vol. VI, tit. II, p. 1931.

10 Conc. Plen. Balt. II, Liber III, p. 15.

a Mass which is said at a privileged altar.[11] But long before this prohibition had been incorporated into the Code, moralists had found a way to curcumvent this law. "It is forbidden," they said, "to demand a larger stipend for a Mass which is celebrated at a privileged altar; but it is not forbidden to say at a privileged altar those Masses only for which an unusually large stipend has been offered spontaneously." [12]

In some instances, the Holy See has relaxed the stringent law on traffic in stipends by means of particular indults and responses. Thus Rome has reluctantly permitted a certain Bishop to appoint an official collector of stipends, whose commission it reduced from five to three per cent.[13]

In another case, the Congregation of the Council tolerated the usage whereby a pastor gave his curates the usual (Low Mass?) stipend for a High Mass and kept the balance as partial payment of the curates' board, where such was the diocesan arrangement.[14] Before the Code, the Holy See tolerated the practice (where the ancient custom obtained), in virtue of which a pastor went so far as to demand of his unfortunate curates that they celebrate and apply almost *all* their Masses according to his intention, so that he could keep the stipends for the curates' food and lodging.[15]

Since the Code, a similar case was submitted to the Holy See. Custom obliged the curates in the diocese of Montevideo to comply with an arrangement whereby every pastor gave each of his curates board and lodging, together with a fixed monthly salary of 25 pesos and another sum of 25 pesos for Masses. The curate in turn had to apply all his Masses according to the intention of the pastor, who kept all the stipends. Later there was passed a

11 Canon 918-2, "Pro Missis celebrandis in altari privilegiato nequit sub obtentu privilegii maior exigi Missae eleemosyna."

12 Link, "Mess-Stipendien," p. 197.

13 S. C. C., decr. 18 Mart., 1905; A. S. C., XXXVIII, 79-81.

14 Link, "Mess-Stipendien," p. 227-h. A. S. S. XXXVII, p. 524; S. C. C., decr. 26 Feb. 1910; A. A. S., II, p. 203.

15 S. C. C., decr. 25 Feb. 1905; A. S. S. XXXVIII, p. 16.

diocesan statute obliging the pastors to give their curates a monthly salary of 25 "pondera" and a daily Mass stipend, so that each curate's monthly income amounted to 50 "pondera" in addition to his board and lodging. The question at issue was whether this custom could be sustained.

The Congregation of the Council replied as follows: [16] "propositam consuetudinem remunerandi coadiutores vicarios tolerari posse. Et ad mentem. Mens autem est, quod Administrator Apostolicus operam navet ut in praxi ponatur statutum dioecesanum vi cuius parochi cooperatoribus suis mercedem solvant 25 ponderum, adiecto quotidie Missae stipendio integro iuxta taxam, ita ut honorarium menstruum summae 50 ponderum coaequetur."

Attention is called to the following point in regard to this decision: the Congregation of the Council ignored the custom of taking stipends for board, and directed its whole attention to the statute prescribing stipends distinct from board and salary. For the Administrator was instructed to have the curates receive a regular monthly salary of 25 "pondera" besides a daily integral Mass stipend (adiecto quotidie Missae stipendio integro iuxta taxam).

To conclude: the most that can be deduced from the decisions before or since the Code, is that the custom of keeping stipends for a curate's board does not violate Canon 827 or Canon 840. But (salva reverentia) no response of the Holy See seems to militate against the contention that a Bishop who compels his curates to pay for their board with the stipends for their Masses thereby violates certain other canons of the Code.[17]

For the Code expressly provides that curates should receive an adequate salary for their work as curates, such as preaching, hearing confessions and visiting the sick.[18] But to apply the fruits of a Mass is not a part

16 S. C. C., 10 Ian. 1920; A. A. S., XII, 70-73.
17 Canons 476 and 831.
18 Canon 476.

of a curate's duties;[19] so to do is his sacerdotal privilege, a privilege recognized by canon law and by all fair-minded Catholics. Canon 824 makes it clear beyond cavil that the Code recognizes the right of every priest to apply the special fruit of his Masses according to his own good pleasure; and no Bishop may lawfully deprive a priest of this right to apply a Mass freely, and consequently to accept stipends over and above the curate's salary.[20] It would be well to ponder the sane advice of Cardinal Gasparri:[21]

"Ceterum S. Sedes, si in aliquibus gravibus circumstantiis Missae celebrationem iubet, eiusdem applicationem exigere non solet. Hanc Sedis Apostolicae prudentiam episcopi imitentur; et nonnisi raro sacerdotibus Missae applicationem imponant, eos stipendio quo forte indigent, privantes."

19 Canon 476, n. 6.

20 Link, "Mess-Stipendien," p. 239, "Auch der Bischof kann gegen das gemeine Recht keine Verpflichtung zur applikation auferlegen."

21 Gasparri, "De Eucharistia," Vol. I, n. 638.

CHAPTER IX

THE NUMBER OF MASSES
OR
CANON 828

The general prohibition of traffic in Mass stipends is followed by a specific law which prescribes that the number of Masses applied must correspond with the number of stipends accepted. Canon 828 reads: "Tot celebran dae et applicandae sunt Missae, quot stipendia etiam exigua data et accepta fuerint." "So many Masses must be said and applied as Mass stipends, even small ones, were offered and accepted." [1]

A Council held at Lambeth in England (Benedict XIV assigns it to the year 1282, whereas Link puts it exactly a century earlier) [2] instructed priests that they could not fulfill their obligation by saying one Mass when they had agreed to say two. The wording of Canon 828 seems to be based on the language which was used by Innocent XII [3] in 1697, and before him by Urban XIII [4] in 1625, viz.: "S. Congregatio (Concilii) [5] sub obstetatione Divini Iudicii mandat, et praecipit, ut absolute tot Missae celebrentur, quot ad rationem attributae eleemosynae praescriptae fuerint." [6]

The following proposition was condemned by Alexander VII, "Non est contra iustitiam, pro pluribus sacrificiis stipendium accipere et sacrificium unum offerre: neque est contra fidelitatem, etiam si promittam, promis-

1 Cf. Woywod, The New Canon Law, p. 167, n. 671.

2 Cf. Benedict XIV, De Missae Sacrificio, lib. 3, cap. XXI, n. 15; Link, p. 206.

3 Cf. Innocentius XII, const. "Nuper," 23 Dec. 1697-4.

4 Cf. Urban VIII, const. "Cum saepe contingat," 1625, Fontes, Vol. I, p. 509, sect. 2.

5 Cf. S. C. C. 21 Jun. 1625, n. 3; Fontes, Vol. I, p. 510.

6 Cf. Fontes, Vol. I, p. 510.

sione etiam iuramento firmato, danti stipendium, quod pro nullo alio offeram." [7] Hence, it is certain that priests who violate Canon 828 sin against justice; and Innocent XII declares expressly that such priests commit a grievous sin and are bound to restitution.[8]

Suppose, however, that a priest agrees to say a hundred Masses for the same intention and then fails to say one of them. Does he commit a mortal sin by the omission of that one Mass? Lehmkuhl said, "No"; for it is an accepted principle of moral theology that he does not sin grievously who fails to fulfill a promise in some detail which in itself is grave enough, but in comparison with the whole thing promised becomes relatively insignificant.[9] Nay, even the omission of an individual Mass (*i. e.*, one that did not belong to a series of Masses) was considered a venial sin only, if the stipend did not constitute grave matter.[10]

Palmieri recognized the seriousness of the obligation which every stipend imposes, but at the same time he perceived that a trivial "alms" of itself could not beget a serious obligation. He concluded that, since the grave duty of saying a Mass for every stipend cannot arise from the value of the money nor from the contract, this duty must originate in the precept of the Church.[11]

These divergent opinions are based on the mistaken notion that Mass stipends constitute or at least resemble a contract of sale (emptio-vinditio). Now Mass stipends, in point of fact, have nothing whatever in common with sales: they belong to that class of innominate contracts which is called "do ut facias." [12]

Such innominate contracts do not imply a comparison

7 Cf. Prop. damn. ab Alex. VII, n. 10 in Decr. S. Inquisit., 24 Sept. 1665; Cf. Denzinger Enchiridion, n. 1110 (981).

8 Cf. Fontes, Vol. I, p. 510, n. 4 ad finem, "Quinimo graviter peccent, et ad restitutionem tenentur."

9 Cf. Noldin, Vol. II, De Praeceptis, n. 215 ad finem, p. 231.

10 Cf. inter alios, Ballerini, Theol. Mor., Vol. IV, n. 102.

11 Cf. Ballerini-Palmieri, Vol. IV, 1012 in nota subiecta; Vermeersch, Epitome, Vol. II, p. 54, nota (1).

12 Cf. Chapter II of this dissertation.

or equality of the things promised.[13] Hence, the gravity of the responsibility which such a contract imposes on either of the contracting parties must be determined by the nature of the thing which that party agrees to give or to do; and the seriousness or triviality of either party's stipulation has nothing whatever to do with the gravity of the other party's obligation.

Concretely, the person who requests a Mass assumes the duty of giving the priest the prescribed amount of money; and this duty is more or less serious, according as the diocesan stipend approaches to, or recedes from, being relatively grave matter for the celebrant of the Mass. The priest, nevertheless, assumes the ever-serious obligation of applying the inestimable fruits of the Mass for the intention of the giver. Consequently, a priest who fails to say a Mass for every single stipend is bound under pain of mortal sin, not to restore a trifling sum of money, but to make restitution by having the proper number of Masses celebrated by himself or by others and having those invaluable Masses applied according to the intention of each person who gave a stipend.[14]

Still a man may insert into his will a bequest for Masses, but specify such a small stipend for each Mass that no priest will accept the bequest. Formerly, the Bishop could reduce the number of Masses, in order that the request of the legator might be fulfilled as nearly as possible.[15] The Code, however, has taken away from the Bishops all such powers of reduction and has reserved this reduction of Mass stipends to the Holy See.[16]

On the contrary, a person who hands the priest some money and says to him, "Remember me at Mass" or "Say a prayer for my intention in your Mass," does not

13 Cf. Vermeersch, Epitome Juris Canonici, Vol. II, p. 54, not. 1.

14 Cf. Blat, Liber III, De Rebus, p. 1. De Sacramentis, p. 155. E contra vid, Amer. Eccl. Review, July 1921, Vol. XXI, p. 923. "For in a bilateral contract do stipendium ut applices Missam ad meam intentionem, the obligation should be equally grave for both contracting parties."

15 Cf. Zamboni, S. C. C. 19 Aug. 1786; 16 Aug. 1794, d. 5; n. 58, 61.

16 Cf. Canon 1517—2 ad finem.

give the priest a Mass stipend in the canonical sense of the term; and so the recipient of that gift is free to apply the Mass for another intention, for which he has accepted a regular stipend.[17]

The offerings which are made by the faithful on All Souls' Day form a sort of exception to this rule. There are other occasions on which a priest may lawfully accept the whole collection or donation, *e. g.*, on the feast of a society's patron saint, or at a First Mass.[18] And if the spiritual director of the society engages another priest to say the Mass, the substitute is not entitled to anything more than the diocesan stipend.[19]

17 Cf. S. C. C. 21 Jan. 1682; Cf. Link, Mess-Stipendien, p. 209.

18 Benedict XIV, Institutiones, LVI, n. 7.

19 Vermeersch, Epitome Iuris Canonici, Vol. II, p. 57. "Ipse c. 840 sinit ut retineatur excessus supra taxam dioecesanam si certo constet excessum intuitu personae datum fuisse, ita ut non sit formalis pars stipendii."

CHAPTER X

THE PERPETUITY OF MASS STIPENDS
OR
CANON 829

The canon which prescribes a Mass for each stipend is followed by a corollary to the effect that even the inculpable loss of a stipend does not free a priest from the obligation of celebrating a corresponding Mass. Canon 829 reads, "Licet sine culpa illius qui onere celebrandi gravatur, Missarum eleemosynae iam preceptae perierint, obligatio non cessat." "If the Mass stipends once accepted are lost, though without the fault of him who has the duty to say the Masses, the obligation does not cease." [1]

A priest deposits in a reliable bank the money which was given to him for saying fifty Masses. A week later the bank fails. The priest loses his stipends through no fault of his own (sine culpa). Another priest carelessly carries in his pocket a sum of money which he has accepted as stipends for Masses. Later, the money is lost or stolen—evidently through his own fault (cum culpa). Both priests are bound to say the proper number of Masses, even though their money has disappeared. That is the meaning of Canon 829.

This law might seem to impose an unjust burden on the first priest. Mature reflection, however, will show that Canon 829 is a just law, founded upon Roman law [2] and upon the very nature of Mass stipends.[3] In Roman law, either party to an innominate contract could sue the other party for performance or else regain what he had given.

1 Woywod, The New Canon Law, p. 167, n. 672.

2 Dig. 12, 4, 5, pr. 1 and 2; Code 4, 6, 10; Code 4, 64, 4. Cf. Sherman, Roman Law, Vol. II, p. 326, 760.

3 Arendt, De laesione, etc., p. 1.

Likewise, it seems that according to canon law the giver of a stipend has a right to demand either the money or the celebration and application of a Mass.[4]

Noldin,[5] indeed, teaches that the priest who fails to say the stipulated Mass must restore the stipend. But in the same paragraph he adds that the money perishes for its sacerdotal owner. It is hard to reconcile these two statements. For the priest is bound to fulfill his part of the contract, *i. e.*, to apply the special fruits of the Holy Sacrifice for the prescribed intention; but if the money belongs to the priest, if he is its owner, then he is not to restore that money. Perhaps a distinction will reconcile Noldin's apparently contradictory tenets: if the Mass can no longer be said for the prescribed intention (*e. g.*, success in an examination which is now over), then the priest must refund the money; otherwise, he must say the Mass.

Canon 829 mentions only the duty of celebrating a Mass; for in many instances, a priest accepts an offering for the celebration as distinct from the application of the Holy Sacrifice. Since the word "celebrandi" prescinds from the application of the Mass, the legislator has not used the technical term stipend (stipendium), but has inserted into Canon 829 the generic term "eleemosyna." It is hardly necessary to add that if a priest who has contracted for the mere celebration of a Mass is bound to fulfill his contract, a fortiori the priest who has engaged to apply as well as celebrate a Mass is bound by Canon 829 to live up to his contract.[6]

The canon under consideration applies only to stipends which have been received: "eleemosynae iam perceptae." A priest to whom offerings are sent by private messenger or through the mail, is not responsible for those offerings until he has received them; and he is not bound to say Masses in return for them until he has accepted them.[7]

For example, Father A agrees to forward for Father

4 Gasparri, "De Eucharistia," Vol. I, n. 584.
5 Noldin, De Sacramentis, p. 212; n. 184.
6 Blat, Liber III, De Rebus, pars. 1, p. 155.
7 Cappello, De Sacramentis, Vol. I, p. 545, n. 679.

B ten stipends by registered mail to Father C. On the voyage to Europe the letter containing the ten dollar bill is lost. Father A is not responsible for the money or the Masses, because he, the agent or "mandatarius," has taken the necessary precaution of registering the letter. Father C is not responsible, because he has not received the stipends. Father B, however, is bound to celebrate and apply the ten Masses; for he has accepted the money (Canon 828), he is the "mandans" and "dominus," and he is responsible for the stipends and the Masses until they are accepted by another priest.[8]

Canon 1509 reveals another aspect of Canon 829, by saying that Mass stipends are not subject to prescription. The Ius Civile recognized for Roman citizens the so-called "usucapio" or mode of acquiring a clear title after lapse of time. The Ius Gentium protected the title of non-citizens through the "possessio longi temporis."[9] In Justinean law,[10] the obsolete "usucapio and possessio longi temporis" became consolidated under the general term of "praescriptio."

Prescription either confers a right or extinguishes an obligation by lapse of time.[11] After a period fixed by law, the courts refuse to recognize the title of the old owner, in order to limit the number of law suits.[12] Certain things, however, are not subject to prescription. Thus, Roman law exempted dotal property during marriage[13] and the property of wards during their guardianship.[14] Canon law exempts the boundaries of dioceses, ecclesiastical benefices and particularly Mass stipends.[15] Therefore, the fact that several years have elapsed since a priest accepted a stipend does not excuse him from saying the Mass.[16]

8 Canon 839.
9 Sherman, Roman Law, Vol. II, p. 216-646.
10 Code 7, 31; Code 7, 39, 8.
11 Inst. 2, 6.
12 Dig. 41, 10, 5—"Ut aliquis litium finis esset."
13 Code 5, 12, 30.
14 Code 7, 35, 3.
15 Canon 1509.
16 Canon 829 and Canon 1509, n. 5.

CHAPTER XI

THE NUMBER OF STIPENDS
OR
CANON 830

The precept of saying as many Masses as there are stipends gives rise to a difficulty when neither the number of Masses nor the amount of each stipend has been fixed by the giver of the money. This difficulty is solved by Canon 830, which says that the faithful are presumed to ask for a number of Masses at the rate of the diocesan stipend.

Canon 830 reads thus: "Si quis pecuniae summam obtulerit pro Missarum applicatione, non indicans earundem numerum, his supputetur secundum eleemosynam loci in quo oblator morabatur, nisi aliam fuisse eius intentionem legitime praesumi debeat." [1] "If a person has offered a certain sum of money for Holy Masses to be said, without indicating how many Masses he desires, the number must be reckoned according to the ordinary stipends customary in the place where the giver of them lived, unless circumstances are such that it must be lawfully presumed that his intention was different." [2]

Canon 830 repeats in substance the old law which was promulgated by Innocent XII in 1697, "si tribuens eleemosynam numerum Missarum celebrandarum non praescripserit, tunc tot Missas celebrari debere, quot praescripserit Ordinarius secundum morem Civitatis, vel provinciae." [3]

Canon 830 applies to all kind of Mass stipends. Obviously it is intended primarily for manual stipends, which

1 Cf. Canon 830.

2 Cf. Woywod, The New Canon Law, p. 167, n. 673.

3 Cf. Innocentius XII. const. Nuper, 23 Dec. 1697—15, ad 2; Fontes, n. 260.

are either handed to the priest by the faithful or bequeathed to him through the last will of a deceased person.[4] It is applicable to quasi-manual stipends; for a beneficiary who has a founded Mass celebrated by another priest must give that priest no more than the regular diocesan offering,[5] and the presumption is that he intends to bestow no more than he is absolutely obliged to give. In theory, this law applies also to foundations of Masses;[6] but in practice, the number of founded Masses is almost always determined accurately by the founder or may easily be calculated from the wording of the foundation.

As regards manual stipends, the offering for a Low Mass is determined in many dioceses of the United States by custom rather than by statutory law, whereas, the fee for a High Mass or Solemn Mass is minutely regulated by synodal decrees.[7] These regulations suggest the question, "If a person gives fifty dollars for Masses without specifying their number, may the priest conscientiously celebrate two Solemn Masses or ten High Masses instead of fifty Low Masses?"

Apropos of this question, it may be well to bear in mind that the Church prefers a High Mass to a Low Mass. If this is true, then the celebrant of a Solemn Mass receives his portion of the fee, not from any extrinsic title of incidental splendor, but from the intrinsic right conferred on him by the celebration of the Holy Sacrifice as the Church would have him celebrate it. Hence, the celebrant's portion of the offering for a Solemn Mass constitutes a Mass stipend in the strict sense of the term.[8] Consequently, if someone gives a

4 Cf. Blat. Liber II, Pars. 1; De Sacramentis, p. 156.

5 Cf. decr. S. C. C., "Ut debita," 11 maii, 1904, n. 15. A. S. S., Vol. XXXVI, p. 676; Hilling, Die Mess-Stipendien und Stolgebühren, p. 13.

6 Cf. Canon 1545.

7 Cf. Chapter XII of this book, p. 94.

8 Cf. Blat, Liber II, pars. I, p. 157. "Ordinarii loci est manualem Missarum stipem—definire quoad stipis quantitatem, forsan diversam pro civitate ac pro ruralibus parochiis, pro Missis lectis vel cantatis," etc.

priest fifty dollars "for Masses" without in any way indicating the number, the priest may lawfully celebrate and apply two Solemn Masses rather than fifty Low Masses —provided always that he need not presume other intentions on the part of the giver.[9]

In like manner, a High Mass (Missa Cantata) is one which does not attain to the Church's ideal, but which approaches more nearly to that ideal than does the Low Mass. It follows that the celebrant of a High Mass should look upon the usual offering for it as nothing more than a formal stipend. Therefore, since Canon 830 makes no distinction between stipends for Low Masses and offerings for High Masses, the priest who is given "fifty dollars for Masses" may, with due regard for other presumed intentions, apply ten High Masses rather than fifty Low Masses.[10]

"If a person offers a sum of money for Masses and does not specify whether he wants Low Masses or High Masses, one opinion holds that only Low Masses must be said for the money, but there is no substantial reason given for this opinion, for if the will of the donor is not explicitly or implicitly expressed in favor of Low Masses, it is difficult to see why the priest should be bound to say only Low Masses, especially when it is known that in the church of the priest to whom the money for Masses was given, the Masses are almost all High Masses. But even apart from such a circumstance there seems to be no necessity of applying the money for Low Masses only, provided, as already said, that there is no indication of a preference for Low Masses on the part of the donor." [11]

9 Cf. Pallotini, "Collectio Resolutionum S. Cong. Concilii," Tomus XIII, p. 607, n. 107. "Unde in taxando stipendio (Missarum) attendendae sunt circumstatiae loci ac temporis et *qualitatis* Missarum, cum maius stipendium sit taxandum pro una Missa, quam pro alia, nempe pro solemni ac cantata, quam pro non solemni," n. 3 in Ianuen. Oratorii die 15 Iulii 1848—Ut. Cf. Note (8).

10 Cf. Woywood, "Regulations, etc., sub-title "Mass Stipends" in The Homiletic and Pastoral Review, June, 1921; Vol. XXI, No. 9, p. 812.

11 Cf. Woywod in the Homiletic & Pastoral Reviews, June, 1921, Vol. XXI, No. 9, p. 812.

Before a priest decides to apply a few Solemn Masses or Missae Cantatae in preference to many low ones, it is imperative for him to take into consideration the proviso contained in the canon of which this chapter treats. That proviso subordinates the local rate of stipends to the presumed intention of the giver: "nisi aliam fuisse eius intentionem legitime praesumi debeat."

A few examples might clarify this principle. If the giver of the money asks, "What is the usual offering for a Mass?" He is presumed to expect as many Masses as his sum of money will yield ordinary stipends. If he is wont to give a certain sum (*e. g.*, two dollars instead of one), then he may be presumed to be requesting Masses at that rate.[12] Finally, people who are bound to a priest by bonds of consanguinity (*e. g.*, a rich uncle) or friendship or gratitude (*e. g.*, convert after a long period of instruction): these may well be presumed to give larger stipends than usual.[13] The language of such people must be studied carefully. If a person tells the priest, "Say a couple of Masses for me," the recipient could hardly be blamed for interpreting the request literally, and therefore celebrating and applying two Masses, for two make a couple. Again, if the request is worded "say a few Masses," two would not suffice and ten would be too many. Hence, "a few" would probably mean a minimum of four Masses.

But the words "some Masses" must generally be taken to mean "as many Masses as I am entitled to." But even in this supposition, there might be cases in which "some" means "a few."

In this, as in similar perplexities, the wish of the giver can be learned from the person who makes the request and from the manner in which he pronounces his words, rather than from the words themselves.

Canon 830 states that the amount of the stipend is to be regulated by the law of the place where the giver of the money is sojourning. This regulation differs con-

12 Cf. Cappello, De Sacramentis, Vol. I, p. 545, n. 678.

13 Cf. Geier, De Missarum Stipendiis, p. 81.

siderably from the old canon law. Before the Code, the number of Masses depended upon the offering which was prescribed for the diocese where the Mass was celebrated; since the Code, it depends upon the regulations in the diocese of the giver's sojourn.[14]

In other words, Canon 830 does not refer to the giver's domicile nor to the place where the Mass is said, but only to the place where the contract is made.[15]

14 Cf. Blat, Lib. III, pars. I, De Sacramentis, p. 156.
15 Cappello, "De Sacramentis," Vol. I, n. 678, p. 545.

CHAPTER XII

THE DIOCESAN STIPEND
OR
CANON 831

Having referred to an offering whose amount depends upon diocesan statute or local custom rather than personal caprice, the Code logically proceeds to tell how this legal fee originates and whom it affects. Canon 831 states the law in the following words:

"Ordinarii loci est manualem Missarum stipem in sua dioecesi definire per decretum, quantum fieri potest, in dioecesana Synodo latum; nec sacerdoti licet ea maiorem exigere.

"Ubi desit Ordinarii decretum, servetur consuetudo dioecesis.

"Etiam religiosi, licet exempti, circa stipem manualem stare debent decreto Ordinarii loci aut dioecesis consuetudini." [1]

It is the right of the local Ordinary to fix the amount of the stipend, which should, as far as possible, be done in the diocesan synod; the priest may not demand a larger stipend than has been fixed by the law of the Bishop.

"Where there is no law of the Bishop fixing the stipend, the custom of the diocese should be followed.

"All religious, also the exempt ones, are obliged to observe the law of the Bishop, or the custom of the diocese, concerning Mass stipends." [2]

Before the Council of Trent, canon law did not concern itself with the amount of money in any manual or founded stipend. Nevertheless, for centuries the proverbial offering for a Mass had been the "denarius." [3]

1 Cf. Canon 831 in C. I. C.

2 Cf. Woywod, The New Canon Law, n. 674, p. 167.

3 Cf. Link, Mess-Stipendien, p. 153.

The Council of Trent contented itself with a vague prohibition of simony.[4] In 1697, Innocent XII wrote:[5] "Censuit (S. C. Concilii), ubi nullam certam eleemosynam Testator reliquit, esse ab Episcopo praescribendam eleemosynam congruam, quae respondeat oneribus Missarum celebrandarum, secundum morem Civitatis, vel Provinciae."

In the following year the Congregation of the Council issued a decree, which is repeated substantially in Canon 831. That portion of the decree, which is to the point, says,[6] "Attendendam esse consuetudinem loci vel legem synodalem, quatenus adsit, sin minus, statuendam esse per episcopum eleemosynam competentem eius arbitrio."

An Ordinary, according to Canon 198 / 1, is any one of the following prelates: the Pope, a resident Bishop in his own territory, an abbot or prelate "nullius," an Administrator of a diocese, or Vicar Apostolic, a prefect Apostolic and the major Superiors of religious (*e. g.*, Provincial). The Ordinary of the place, according to Canon 198 / 2, may be any of these officials, except the religious Superiors.

Canon 831 restricts the power of fixing the rate of stipends to the Ordinary of the place, thereby excluding the Superiors of religious; for the third section of this canon says expressly that in regard to Mass stipends, exempt religious must obey the local Ordinary.[7]

The canon under discussion gives the Bishop the right to regulate the amount of manual stipends; quasi-manual stipends are governed by the Canon 840 / 2. As regards founded Masses, Canon 1545 gives the local Ordinary the

4 Cf. Conc. Trid., sess. 22, de obser. et evitandis in celebr. missae.

5 Cf. Innocentius XII, const. "Nuper," 23 Dec. 1697,-15 ad. 5. Fontes, n. 260.

6 Cf. S. C. C. Decr. Aprutina, 15 Nov. 1698, ad. 1. Pallottini, "Collectio," Vol. XIII, n. 120, p. 609.

7 Cf. Cappello, De Sacramentis, Vol. I, n. 671, 1°, p. 538.

same right concerning founded stipends as Canon 831 does concerning *manual stipends.*[8]

Since the term "Ordinary of the place" includes Vicars and prefects Apostolic as well as abbots "nullius," the correlative expression "diocese" includes vicariates and prefectures Apostolic[9] as well as abbeys and prelatures "nullius."[10]

What is the force of the word "definere" in Canon 831? It certainly means that the priest may not *demand* more than the sum specified.[11] If he wishes, he may ordinarily accept less. If he and the person who asks for a Mass have agreed upon the sum to be offered, this canon does not apply.[12] But if no such agreement has been reached, then the priest is entitled to the amount fixed by the Bishop, the synod or the custom of the place.[13] Incidentally, the phrase "custom of the place" is more precise than the expression, "custom of the diocese"; for in large dioceses where circumstances vary considerably in different localities, the Bishop may establish a legal rate for one portion of the diocese (*e. g.*, the Episcopal City or the metropolis of the State) and another sum for the rest of the diocese or for the country parishes.[14]

The Bishop's decree constitutes a real law which ought to be passed in the diocesan synod and in accordance with Canons 360 and 362.[15] Still, the clause "quantum fieri potest" indicates that the obligation has no bearing upon the validity of the Bishop's decree, but only on its liceity. In fact, any just cause will permit the Ordinary to establish the rates for Masses without awaiting or convoking a synod;[16] for, after all, even

8 Cf. Canon 1545: "Loci Ordinarii est normas praescribere de dotis quantitate infra quam pia fundatio admitti nequeat et de eius fructibus rite distribuendis."

9 Cf. Canon 294—1.

10 Cf. Canon 215—2.

11 Cf. Canon 831—2 (which says "nec sacerdoti licet ea majorem exigere").

12 Cf. Canon 832.

13 Cf. Blat, Lib. III, pars. I, p. 157.

14 Cf. Cappello, De Sacramentis, Vol. I, n. 671, par. 3, p. 539.

15 Cf. Blat, Lib. III, pars. 1, De Sacramentis, p. 157.

16 Cf. Cappello, De Sacramentis, Vol. I, n. 671, 4°, p. 539.

in the synod itself, the sole legislator of the diocese is the Bishop.[17]

In default of an episcopal decree, recourse is had to custom. The use of the legal term "consuetudo" in preference to the non-technical expression "mos" of Canon 824 shows that the custom has the force of law; and therefore, it must be at least forty years old and morally co-extensive with the diocese. This custom, nevertheless, does not abridge the Bishop's power of increasing or decreasing the rate of the diocesan stipend according to his prudent judgment of the circumstances which obtain in his diocese.[18] Nay, with due regard for distributive justice, the Bishop may establish for even one parish or priest a special fee whose rate is higher or lower than the usual one.[18]

All the secular and non-exempt religious priests of the diocese are bound to obey the Bishop's decree, because they are his subjects, even the exempt religious (except the Jesuits [18b]) must obey his order, because Canon 831 / 3 expressly mentions Mass stipends as one of the things in which regulars are not exempt from episcopal jurisdiction; and visitors are bound to comply with the diocesan decree, because Canon 830 subjects Mass stipends to the legal adage "locus dirigit actum."

When the Code say "religiosi *stare* debent decreto Ordinarii," it forbids religious to go about seeking stipends lower than the legal fee, but it does not deprive them of their right to accept isolated offerings of small amount, according to natural law and Canon 832.

An offering of the amount prescribed by law or custom as the diocesan stipend for a Low Mass, entitles the giver to have a Low Mass celebrated and its special fruit applied to him by some priest in any part of the world within a vaguely defined period of time. Mutatis

17 Cf. Canon 362: "Unicus est in Synodo legislator Episcopus."

18 Cf. Cappello, De Sacramentis, Vol. I, n. 672, pp. 540-541.

18b Cf. Gasparri, "De Eucharistia," Vol. I, p. 398, n. 550. Cappello, "De Sacramentis," Vol. I, p. 540, n. 672, footnote 46. Gury-Ballerini, Compendium Theol. Mor., Vol. II, pp. 261-264. Cappello and Gury are members of the Society of Jesus.

mutandis, the same is true of the synodal tax for a High Mass or a Solemn Mass.

If people insist that the Mass be celebrated at nine o'clock next Tuesday morning in St. Josaphat's Church, and that this Mass for Mary Jones be advertised at every parochial Mass on the preceding Sunday, then the Bishop may prescribe and priests may demand an excess above the ordinary stipend for this inconvenience, risk and publicity, which are extrinsic to the Sacrifice as such.[19] Vermeersch,[20] unlike Cappello,[21] points out the distinction between the formal stipend for the mere application of the Mass and the material stipend or total offering for incidentals of time, person and place.

Vermeersch [22] and Cappello [23] disagree on the question whether he who demands more than the usual tax is guilty of simony. Vermeersch's opinion seems to be the preferable one: such exaction is unjust but not simoniacal. Vermeersch does not say that such a person always commits a mortal sin; but he admits that the person is bound to restore the excess.[24] Cappello boldly declares that it is grievously sinful to demand repeatedly more than the statutes or custom permits.[25] Concerning the obligation of restitution, it would seem that the priest is bound to restore the unjust excess to the giver sub gravi or sub levi, according as that excess money constitutes relatively grave or light matter for the giver of the stipend.[26]

Turning now from universal to particular law, the reader learns that in 1810 the Bishops of the United

19 Cf. Hilling, "Die Mess-Stipendien und Stolgebühren," p. 44. Cf. Cappello, "De Sacramentis," Vol. I, n. 672, ad. 3.

20 Cf. Vermeersch, Epitome Iuris Canonici, Vol. II, n. 197, par. 3 ad finem, p. 57: "Ipse canon 840 sinit ut retineatur excessus supra taxam dioecesanam si certo constet excessum intuitu personae datum fuisse, ita ut non sit formalis pars stipendii."

21 Cf. Cappello, De Sacramentis, Vol. I, n. 672, 3, p. 541.

22 Cf. Vermeersch, Epitome Iuris Canonici, Vol. II, n. 10, p. 6.

23 Cf. Cappello, De Sacramentis, Vol. I, n. 676, p. 543.

24 Cf. Vermeersch, Epitome Iuris Canonici, Vol. II, n. 10, p. 6.

25 Cf. Cappello, De Sacramentis, Vol. I. n. 673, p. 541, sqq et. auctores ibi citatos: e. g. Benedict XIV, de M. Sac., C. 3, c. 21.

26 Cf. Cappello, l. c., n. 669.

States made a half-dollar the canonical stipend for a Low Mass in this country. For curiosity's sake, their exact words will bear quotation: "Habita ratione pretii ciborum caeterorumque ad vitam necessariorum in dies crescentis, retributio pro una privata Missa celebranda taxatur ad dimidiam partem nummi Americani." [27]

As late as 1856, the diocese of Richmond, Va., had a synodal fee of only fifty cents.[28] Albany,[29] Baltimore,[30] Boston,[31] New York [32] and San Francisco [33] have established a synodal tax of one dollar for a private Mass. The dollar stipend, which was introduced by law or custom a half-century ago,[34] still exists in most parts of the United States of America.[35]

In St. Louis, Mo., and in the Philippine Islands, the usual offering is two dollars. For the archdiocese of Philadelphia the following scale has been established by diocesan statute: [36]

"Taxae manent quales antea fuerint in nostra et in plerisque hujus regionis dioecesibus.

"Pro Missa Funebri Solemni: Scutata viginti quinque.

"Pro Missa Funebri Cantata: Scutata quindecim.

"Pro Missa privata et exequiis: Scutata quinque."

27 Cf. Concilia Provincilia Baltimori, p. 23, n. 7. "Ex Articulis Ecclesiasticae Disciplinae quos Archiepiscopus Baltimorensis et Episcopi Americae Foederatae communi consensu anno 1810 sanxerunt."

28 Cf. First Synod of Richmond, 1856, n. 48.

29 Cf. Fourth Synod of Albany, 1887, n. 195.

30 Cf. Eighth Synod of Baltimore, 1875, n. 78.

31 Cf. Constitutiones Dioecesanae, 1886, n. 158.

32 Cf. Fifth Synod of New York, 1886, n. 201.

33 Cf. Diocesan Synod of San Francisco, 1867, n. 25.

34 Cf. Smith, Elements of Ecclesiastical Law, Vol. I, p. 317, n. 593, 7th Ed., 1887, "In the United States, the honorary (i. e., the stipend) is generally one dollar."

35 Cf. Augustine, A Commentary, Vol. IV, p. 190, Ed. of 1920, ". . . ten Masses would have to be said in our country, where the usual stipend is one dollar for a Mass."

36 Cf. Statuta Provincialia et Dioecesana, p. 49.

CHAPTER XIII

GENEROUS AND TENUOUS STIPENDS OR CANON 832

Whilst Canon 831 tells what every priest may demand for saying Mass, Canon 832 tells what any priest may accept for celebrating and applying the Eucharistic Sacrifice. The canon is couched in the following language, "Sacerdoti fas est oblatam ultro maiorem stipem pro Missae applicatione accipere, et, nisi loci Ordinarius prohibuerit, etiam minorem." [1] In other words, "The priest may accept a larger stipend, if voluntarily offered; and, unless the Ordinary has forbidden it, he may accept a smaller one." [2]

This juridical doctrine, which the Code has elevated to the dignity of an explicit law, was taught by an eminent canonist and defended by him on the ground that as a rule the law cannot limit the liberality of priest or people.[3]

Long before the Code came into being, all priests who had accepted stipends smaller than the one prescribed by the Ordinary were obliged by canon law to celebrate Mass for these stipends.[4] Nevertheless, both the old and the new law give the Bishop the right of forbidding priests to accept smaller stipends than he has

1 Cf. Canon 832, C. I. C.

2 Cf. Woywod, The New Canon Law, n. 675, p. 168.

3 "Quae tamen taxatio numquam ita fieri potest, quin abundantius concedi a sacrificium petentibus, et minus admitti a sacrificantibus possit . . . quia lex et consuetudo taxams stipendium non prohibet, nec pronibere regulariter potest usum, et exercitium liberalitatis tam ex parte concedentium stipendium quam ex parte sacerdotum celebrantium." Schmalzgrueber, Jus Ecclesiasticum Universum, pars. V, tit. XLI, p. 487, n. 101.

4 Cf. Innocentius XII, const. Nuper, 23 Dec. 1697, 15, ad. 3; Fontes, Vol. I, p. 513.

established.[5] If the Bishop expressly forbids priests to take such small stipends, regular, no less than secular priests, are bound to conform to this diocesan norm, because of the harm which would otherwise accrue to the rest of the clergy.[6] The Bishop, however, cannot prevent any priest from saying Mass gratuitously[7] or from accepting any sum which is offered voluntarily over and above the ordinary stipend.[8]

It is a mistake to think or to teach that if people cannot afford to give the priest a dollar, he is not allowed to accept less than that amount and must either say the Mass for nothing or else refuse their petition entirely. As long as the Bishop has not expressly forbidden the clergy to accept less than the synodal tax, the priests may accept whatever sum is offered to them and say Mass for the intention of the giver.

The question arises, "How can an American Bishop proceed against Canadian priests who solicit Mass stipends at the rate of fifty cents each by means of circular letters sent to Catholics in the United States?" If no synodal statute or episcopal decree against this solicitation existed at the time when the letters were circulated, the Bishop cannot prosecute the priests; for he cannot make his injunction retroactive[9] any more than a civil legislature can pass an ex post facto law.[10] If he can cite a pre-existing diocesan law against such solicitation, the Bishop can argue that by a fiction of law the priests were present in his diocese when they sent the letters into it; consequently he can put them

5 Cf. S. C. C. S. Severini, 16 iul. 1689; Cf. Canon 832; Cf. Pallottini, Collectio, Tomus XIII, p. 609, n. 119.

6 Cf. S. C. C. Ordinis Minorum Conventualium 8 maii, 1905; Cf. A. S. S. Vol. 38, p. 14.

7 Cf. Hilling, Die Mess-Stipendien u. Stolgebühren, p. 36, footnote.

8 Cf. S. C. C. jan. 16, 1649.

9 Cf. Canon 10, "Leges respiciunt futura, non praeterita, nisi nominatim in eis de praeteritis caveatur."

10 Cf. The Constitution of the United States of America, Article I, Section 10, Clause 1: "No State shall pass any bill of attainder, ex post facto law," etc.

on trial[11] and sentence them to some ecclesiastical punishment without the compulsory co-operation of the priests' own Ordinary.[12] The usual mode of procedure in America would be to submit the whole case to the Canadian Bishop.[12]

What punishment can a Bishop licitly inflict upon those who solicit stipends at a lower rate than the diocesan statutes permit? Canon 2408 does not answer the question, because that canon refers to Canon 1507, but not to Canon 832. Nor does Canon 2324 apply; for it refers only to Canons 827, 828 and 840. The answer is found in the "blanket clause," which covers a multitude of crimes: Canon 832 is sanctioned by Canon 2222, which states that ecclesiastical Superiors can inflict a suitable punishment for any transgression against any canon in the Code.[13]

11 Canon 1566.
12 Canon 1561.
13 Cf. Canon 2222.

CHAPTER XIV

INCIDENTAL OBLIGATIONS
OR
CANON 833

Whereas the canons hitherto explained have been concerned principally with the application of the Mass's fruit, the canon which forms the subject of this chapter deals with non-essential duties regarding the celebration of the Holy Sacrifice. Canon 833 puts the law as follows:

"Praesumitur oblatorem petiisse solam Missae applicationem; si tamen oblator expresse aliquas circumstantias in Missae celebratione servandas determinaverit, sacerdos, eleemosynam acceptans, eius voluntati stare debet."

"It is presumed that the one who offers the stipend only requests the application of Holy Mass; if, however, he has explicitly stipulated certain circumstances for its celebration, the priest who accepts the stipend must fulfill the conditions made by the one who offered the stipend." [1]

Since the law itself takes it for granted that the giver of a stipend expects nothing more than the application of a Mass, the burden of proof rests upon the person who makes the offering. The presumption is a presumption of law only,[2] and therefore admits of direct proof to the contrary.[3]

If then a person desires something more than the mere application of a Mass, he must explicitly (not implicitly or tacitly) make known in writing or by word of mouth the further obligations which he wishes to impose upon the celebrant. Thus he may ask that the

1 Cf. Woywod, The New Canon Law, p. 168, n. 676.

2 Cf. Blat, Liber III, pars. 1, p. 158.

3 Cf. Canones 1825-1826.

Mass be said at an appointed hour (*e. g.*, the eight o'clock Mass) or on a particular day (next Sunday), or in a certain church (his own parish church), or for an extraordinary reason (a Nuptial Mass on the silver jubilee), or with special ceremonies (a Requiem or "Black Mass," with or without the catafalque).

As a rule, the Priest who accepts a stipend is not obliged to do anything more than his contract canonically calls for. Hence, for many obligations beyond that of saying a Mass at some reasonably convenient time, the priest may lawfully demand from an extrinsic title some remuneration over and above the ordinary offering. If this surplus is not forthcoming, he may reject the stipend and refuse to celebrate the Mass.[3b]

But if he, undertsanding the giver's request, accepts the usual offering, then he is bound by Canon 833 to live up to his agreement by complying with all stipulations regarding the time, place, and kind of Mass to be said. Concerning the seriousness of this obligation, Gury-Ballerini [4] teach that the giver is supposed to be seriously unwilling to cede his rights on these points.

It is not sinful to celebrate in one place a Mass which should have been said in another, provided that the purpose for which the place was specified is not thus frustrated. For instance, if a man prescribes that the Mass for his deceased wife be said at the main altar of the parish church, because that altar is a privileged altar: the celebrant who enjoys personally the right of a privileged altar may offer the Mass for that woman at the side altar of the same or any other church.[4a]

Consequently, if the giver of the stipend prefers the celebration of the Mass on a particular day to the application of the Mass on another day, the stipend must be restored to him if the Mass has not been said at the time and place agreed upon.[4] But this restitution obliges "sub levi" at most.[4b]

3b Cf. Amer. Eccl. Review, Vol. 19, p. 640; Cf. Cappello, Vol. I, n. 672-3.

4 Cf. Gury-Ballerini, Compendium Theologiae Moralis, Vol. 2, p. 259, n. 376, Quaer, 16.

4a Cf. De Lugo, De S. Eucharistiae, Disp. 21, sect. 2, n. 39.

4b Cf. p. 93 (Chapter XII) of this dissertation.

Or a curate agrees for a dollar stipend to celebrate a Nuptial Mass one the day of a couple's silver jubilee. But when the joyous day arrives, he finds that the sexton has set up the black vestments as usual; and so he deliberately says the Mass of the Dead.[6] That curate thereby commits a mortal sin; for he has sorely offended the bridal pair, not indeed by failing to apply the Mass to them, but by neglecting his secondary, though essential, duty of celebrating that Mass in white vestments and according to the rubrics of that special votive Mass.[7]

This example makes it clear that no treatise on stipends would be complete without a short digression on the subject of votive Masses, which have exerted such a strong influence on the development of stipends. Votive Masses are those which do not correspond with the office of the day.[9] They owe their popularity to the teaching that special formulae have a greater efficacy than general prayers, and to special devotions in honor of particular saints or mysteries.

If a votive Mass has been asked for explicitly, the celebrant is bound in justice, but not under penalty of mortal sin, to comply with the request or else to refund the money.[10]

On the contrary, the words, "Mass in honor of the Sacred Heart," or "in honor of the Blessed Virgin or St. Rita," do not necessarily mean a votive Mass, for many people who use these words have never heard of a votive Mass.[11] But if someone says, "I wish you would say a votive Mass in honor of St. Rita," then the Mass of that saint (from the Proprium or the Commune Sanctorum) is to be celebrated as a votive Mass with

5 Cf. Genicot, Theol. Moral., Vol. II, p. 221, n. 233.

6 Cf. A. K. K., 1892, Vol. 68, p. 277, n. 2.

7 Cf. Noldin, De Sacramentis, p. 213, n. 184, 2.

9 Cf. De Herdt, Sacrae Liturgiae Praxis, Tom. I, p. 25; Cf. Link, Mess-Stipendien, p. 314.

10 Link, "Mess-Stipendien," p. 312 and p. 315.

11 Cf. Link, Mess-Stipendien, p. 313.

the appropriate substitution of "Commemoratio" for "festivitas," etc.[12]

The Church obliges a priest to celebrate at a privileged altar every Mass which he has agreed to celebrate there in return for a stipend, for the celebration at a privileged altar is one of the special circumstances referred to in Canon 833. St. Alphonsus defines the privilege in this way: [13] "Privilegium altaris in hoc consistit, ut ex indulgentiis sive fructibus qui sunt in thesauro Ecclesiae liberetur a purgatorio anima, pro qua Missa in illo altari applicatur." Although a Mass at a privileged altar connotes a plenary indulgence, several Masses of this kind may be offered up for the same soul, because the indulgences which are applied by way of suffrage to the poor souls depend for their application and efficacy upon the will of God.[14]

It is no longer necessary to say the Requiem Mass whenever permissible in order to gain the plenary indulgence attached to a privileged altar.[15]

The Code simply repeats the old law when it forbids the clergy to demand a higher stipend for a Mass at a privileged altar.[16] Of course, an easy way to circumvent this legislation would be to say that the surplus is demanded, not for the indulgence or Mass, but for the extrinsic inconvenience of saying Mass at that particular altar.[17]

Pope St. Gregory the Great (590-604) [20] tells that Justus, a monk who had died recently, had asked another monk to offer up thirty Masses for him on thirty con-

12 Cf. Link, Mess-Stipendien, p. 313.

13 Cf. St. Alphonsus, Theol. Mor. lib. 6, n. 9.

14 Cf. Canon 911.

15 S. C. S. Off., 20 Feb., 1913; Cf. Cappello, "De Sacramentis," Vol. I, p. 625, n. 762.

16 Cf. S. C. de prop. Fide, 13 Aug. 1774; Cf. Canon 918, 2, "Pro Missis celebrandis in altari privilegiato nequit, sub obtentu privilegii, maior exigi Missae eleemosyna."

17 Blat, Liber III, pars. 1, p. 312, vs. Augustine, "A Commentary," Vol. IV, p. 369.

20 St. Gregory I; Dialog. lib. 4, cap. 55, "Vade itaque, ab hodiema die diebus triginta continuis offer pro eo Sacrificium," M. P. L., LXXVII, 421.

secutive days. When the series had been completed, Justus appeared to the monk Copiosus, whom he told that he had been released from the torments of Purgatory. Upon computation, it was discovered that the indicated day of his release was the very day on which the thirtieth Mass had been celebrated. Such is the origin of the Gregorian Masses. Centuries later, when abuses had crept in, the Congregation of Rites forbade these travesties; but it did not outlaw the pious custom which St. Gregory had introduced and which still enjoys a widespread popularity.[21]

The essential thing about Gregorian Masses is that a Mass be said every day for thirty consecutive days, *i. e.*, without any interruption, except on the last three days of Holy Week.[22] Hence, two Masses of the same series can not be said by different priests on the same day [23] or by the same priest on Sundays or Christmas.[24] It is not necessary, however, to celebrate these Masses in black vestments.[24]

Since it is not imperative to have the whole series applied by the same celebrant, two priests may divide the Masses between themselves in such a way that one says the first fifteen Masses and the other the remainder.[25] It would be more prudent, however, to agree that each will offer up fifteen Masses, that either will say those which the other cannot celebrate, and that he who breaks the series must assume the whole responsibility.[26] If one of them should forget his agreement and inadvertently make another intention for his Mass, the series would not have to be repeated, because the forgotten intention of the Mass, according to his previous contract, prevails over the subsequent intention, which it nullifies.

Some American Bishops have established a fee of

21 Cf. Benedict XIV; De Missae Sacrificio, p. 236, n. 3.
22 Cf. Benedict XIV; De Missae Sacrificio, n. 3.
23 Cf. Decret, Sancti officii, 12 Dec., 1912; Cf. A. A. S., Vol. V, p. 32.
24 Cf. Augustine, A Commentary, Vol. 4, p. 196.
25 S. C. Indulg; 13 Mar, 1884.
26 S. C. C., 16 Aprilis 1921; A. A. S., XIII, p. 533.

$45 for Gregorian Masses,[27] and for such a series, any priest may lawfully demand more than the usual stipend because of the inconvenience involved and the risk assumed.

If, outside of Holy Week, the Gregorian series has been interrupted for any reason whatsoever, the priest must ask for a concession from the giver of the stipends, or commence the series anew, or ask for a condonation from the Holy See.[28] This is the most probable opinion. Noldin [29] teaches that the priest who has accepted more than the diocesan stipend for these thirty Masses must begin the series anew, whereas the priest who has received only thirty ordinary stipends ($30) may discharge his obligation by saying thirty Masses and celebrating one of them at a privileged altar.

A third opinion, which is not devoid of probability, makes another distinction: if the celebrant is at fault, his confessor should impose the supplementary celebration of several Masses as reparation proportionate to the negligence; but if the contracting priest could not prevent the interruption, he is not obliged to commence the series anew.[30] For example, if a curate fails to say the Gregorian Mass which he has promised to say on Sunday for the pastor, the pastor is not bound to renew the whole series.[31]

27 Cf. Augustine, A Commentary, Vol. 4, p. 196, footnote 38.
28 Cf. Laurent-Dolphin, The Busy Pastor's Guide, p. 63, n. 216.
29 Cf. Noldin, De Sacramentis, pp. 378 and 379, n. 327, b.
30 Cf. Boudinhon, Canoniste Contemporain, May-June, 1917.
31 Cf. Irish Ecclesiastical Record, 1922, Vol. 19, p. 193, 2°.

CHAPTER XV

THE TIME OF CELEBRATION OR CANON 834

After the canon on circumstantial obligations relative to Mass stipends, there follows in logical sequence a law which regulates the most important of these circumstances, viz.: the time when Masses for stipends must be said. Canon 834 proposes this rule of time in the following language:

No. 1. "Missae pro quibus celebrandis tempus ab oblatore expresse praescriptum est, eo omnino tempore sunt celebrandae.

No. 2. "Si oblator nullum tempus pro Missaram manualium celebratione expresse praescripserit:

1° "Missae pro urgenti causa oblatae quamprimum tempore utili sunt celebrandae:

2° "In aliis casibus Missae sunt celebrandae intra modicum tempus pro maiore vel minore Missarum numero.

No. 3. "Qod si oblator arbitrio sacerdotis tempus celebrationis expresse reliquerit, sacerdos poterit tempore quo sibi magis placuerit, eas celebrare, firmo praescripto can. 835."

Woywod has inserted an example into a paragraph which otherwise is nothing but a translation of Canon 834. He says,[1] "Concerning the time when Holy Mass is to be said, the following rules must be observed:

"If the giver of manual stipends did not expressly specify the day, then (1) Masses ordered for an urgent cause must be said as soon as possible, and within the time proper to obtain the purpose, *e. g.*, a Mass said for

1 Cf. Woywod, The New Canon Law, p. 168, n. 677.

a successful examination, which naturally has to be said before the examination takes place; (2) in all other cases Holy Mass must be said within a short time, a longer or shorter period, according to the number of Masses;

"If the giver of the stipend expressly left the time for saying the Holy Masses to the judgment of the priest, he may say them at a time that he finds more convenient. The rule of the following canon, however, must be observed."

In 1625, Urban VIII forbade priests to accept a second stipend or group of stipends before they had discharged all previous obligations.[2] In 1697, Innocent XII tempered this rigid rule by saying that it was not absolute and that a priest who had some stipends on hand could accept still more as long as all the Masses would be said within a short time.[3]

Naturally, the Pontiff's answer that it must be possible to say all the Masses within a short time (modicum tempus), immediately suggested the further question, "What is meant by the expression, 'modicum tempus'?"[4]

The Congregation of the Council answered this question by saying that "infra modicum tempus" meant "infra mensem"; in other words, that no priest might accept more stipends than he could say Masses within a month.[5] As usual, moralists began to explain this response away by teaching that for a recently deceased person the Masses must be said within a month, but for

2 Cf. Urban VIII; const., "Cum saepe contingat," 21 Jun. 1625: "Eleemosynas vero manuales et quotidianas pro Missis celebrandis ita demum iidem accipere possint, si oneribus antea impositis ita satisfecerint, ut nova quoque onera suscipere caleant; alioquin omnino abstineant ab huismodi eleemosynis etiam sponte oblatis, in futurum recipiendis."

3 Cf. Innocentius XII; const. "Nuper," 23 Dec. 1697, No. 15, ad. 11; Fontes, Vol. I, p. 515: "Respondit non prohibere absolute; ac propterea, et si oneribus iam susceptis non satisfecerint, posse tamen nova etiam onera suscipere Missarum celebrandarum, dummodo infra modicum tempus possint omnibus satisfacere."

4 Cf. Innocentius XII, const., "Nuper," 23 Dec. 1697, No. 15, ad 1; Fontes, Vol. I, p. 515.

5 Cf. S. C. C., 17 Julii 1655, "Intelligi infra mensem."

other poor souls the celebration of the Holy Sacrifice could be put off for two or even three months.[6]

The three months' limit had been accepted not only by European moralists, but also by an American canonist,[7] when Rome issued the decree on which the Code's legislation is founded.[8] In that decree, the Congregation of the Council laid down the law that no priest (except the Ordinary or the religious Superior) could accept more "Masses" than he could celebrate in person within a specified time.[8] The same Congregation specified the time in the well known rule: one Mass, one month; a hundred Masses, six months; all Masses, twelve months.[9]

But the priest or other giver must expressly prescribe the time. Hence it would not be sufficient to say, "Please read a Mass for my mother. Tomorrow it will be a year since she died." Nevertheless, it would be advisable to ask such a person whether the Mass must be said on the day suggested; for in his or her mind those words might be equivalent to the more precise request, "Say a Mass tomorrow for my mother." Or, as is generally the case, the words might be intended to convey the wish but not the command that the Holy Sacrifice be offered at the time mentioned, especially if nothing more than the synodal fee is given.

A Mass which is to be said on a feast-day may law-

6 Cf. Gury-Ballerini, Vol. II, p. 252, n. 369: "Gravis sane videri potest dilatio, quae tres menses excedit Ita communiter cum S. Ligorio, contra alios, qui annum integrum requirent. Probabilius autem non peccat graviter Sacerdos, qui Missam promissam intra duos menses celebrat."

7 Cf. Smith, Elements of Ecclesiastical Law, Vol. I, p. 318, n. 594: "A delay exceeding three months is, generally speaking, a mortal sin; nay, as regards Masses for recently deceased persons, a delay of one month constitutes, according to many, a mortal sin."

8 Cf. S. C. C. Decr; "Ut debita," 11 Maii, 1904, n. 1. Cf. A. S. S., Vol. XXXVI, p. 673. "Jamvero de his omnibus S. C. decernit: 1° Neminem posse plus Missarum quaerere et accipere quam celebrare probabiliter valeat intra temporis terminos inferius statutos, et per se ipsum, vel per sacerdotes sibi subditos, si agatur de Ordinario dioecesano aut Praelato regulari."

9 Ibid, n. 2. 2° "Utile tempus ad manualium Missarum obligationes implendas esse mensem pro Missa una, semestre pro centum Missis, et aliud longius vel brevius temporis spatium plus minusve, iuxta maiorem vel minorem numerum Missarum."

fully be celebrated on the following day. For example, if the Tyrolese request a Mass for December 4th in honor of St. Barbara, the priest can discharge his obligation either on the feast of that saint or on the next day.[10]

The first section of Canon 834 applies to all kinds of Masses. The second section mentions manual Masses only; but since quasi-manual stipends are regarded as manual offerings, the rules in Canon 834 / 2 apply also to these "stipendia ad instar manualium." [11]

When Masses are to be said for an urgent reason, the time of their celebration need not be prescribed expressly: it is sufficient to indicate the object of the request.[12] Urgent intentions of frequent occurrence are the following: The spiritual welfare of a dying person; the recovery of health by one whose illness is not chronic; safe delivery; a worthy reception of First Holy Communion; success in an examination, in some business undertaking or in an impending operation. Even a Mass for guidance in the choice of a state in life can be an urgent intention under certain circumstances, such as a mission or a retreat.

Concerning these urgent intentions, the Code imposes upon the celebrant a two-fold obligation:[13] the Mass must be said as soon as possible (quamprimum) and it must be offered up whilst the intention can be realized, or the benefit obtained, *i. e.*, before the event has taken place (tempore utili).[14]

It is a mortal sin of injustice to omit a Mass which has been requested or to defer its celebration until the favor has been granted or can not be granted.[16] There can be no doubt about the gravity of this obligation in

10 Cf. Link, Mess-Stipendien, p. 211.

11 Cf. Noldin, De Sacramentis, p. 219, n. 187-2-d.

12 Cf. Noldin, De Sacramentis, p. 218, n. 187, a.

13 Cf. Canon 834, No. 2, 1° "Missae pro urgenti causa oblatae quamprimum tempore utili sunt celebrandae."

14 Cf. Blat, Liber III; De Rebus, p. 1, De Sacramentis, p. 158—"tempore utili non ad normam can. 35, sed scilicet; quando offerentis intentio consequi potest adhuc effectum."

16 Cf. Noldin, De Sacramentis, p. 218, n. 187, b.

the mind of anyone who understands the contract of Mass stipends.[17]

Canon 834 / 1, 2° gives rise to a question which, from a practical standpoint, is probably the most important one to be discussed in this essay. That number says that Masses for non-urgent reasons must be celebrated within a relatively short time ("intra modicum tempus"), according as the number of Masses is large or small. Must the phrase, "intra modicum tempus," be taken in the sense in which that phrase was interpreted before the Code?[18]

Those who say that "within a short time" still means "within a month for one Mass and within six months for a hundred Masses," appeal to numbers 2 and 4 of Canon 6; and to the objection that number 6 of the same canon renders their contention nugatory, they reply that the old decree is implicitly contained in the new Code.[19] Thus Cappello[20] and Noldin[21] state in clear language that every Mass for an individual manual stipend must be said within a month; and Augustine seems to hold the same opinion.[22]

Vermeersch teaches that the words of the Code *can* be understood according to the rules of the decree "Ut debita"; but he prudently refrains from saying that they *must* be so interpreted.[23] Blat and Prümmer, on the contrary, champion the more lenient opinion which makes

17 Cf. p. 79 of this dissertation.

18 Cf. S. C. C. 17 Iulii 1655—infra modicum tempus "intelligi infra mensem." Cf. S. C. C. decr. "Ut debita," 11 Maii, 1904, n. 2; A. S. S., Vol. 36, p. 673.

19 Cf. Canon 6, 2° "Canones qui ius vetus ex integro referunt, ex veteris iuris anctoritate, atque ideo ex receptis apud probatos auctores interpretationibus, sunt aestimandi." 1° "In dubio num aliquod canonum praescriptum cum veteri iure discrepet, a veteri iure non est recedendum"; 6° "Si qua ex disciplinaribus legibus, quae usque adhuc viguerunt, nec explicite nec implicite in Codice contineatur, ea vim omnem amisisse dicenda est, nisi in probatis liturgicis libris reperiatur, aut lex sit iuris divini sive positivi sive naturalis."

20 Cf. Cappello, "De Sacramentis," Vol. I, p. 548, n. 683—2.

21 Cf. Noldin, "De Sacramentis," p. 218, n. 187—2.

22 Cf. Augustine, "A Commentary," Vol. IV, p. 198, n. 2.

23 Cf. Vermeersch, "Epitome," Vol. II, p. 54, n. 106—4.

the phrase "within a month" a directive counsel, but not a preceptive interpretation of the words "intra modicum tempus" in Canon 834 / 2, n. 2.

Blat's words are well worth quoting:[26] "Si quispiam desideret aliqualem determinationem, poterit recipere ex Decreto, 'Ut debita' ut securam norman *directivam* . . . Sed in Canonis praescripto *non est inserta clausula Dec. 'Ut debita,' sed indefinita:* 'dummodo infra modicum tempus valeant omnibus Missis satisfacere' " . . .

Prümmer declares with even more clearness that the old law has been abrogated and that a priest is no longer bound in conscience to say one Mass within a month or a hundred Masses within six months. He says,[26b] "Quae igitur hac de re statuta fuerant a Decreto "Ut debita" d. 11 Maii 1904, iam amplius non habent nisi valorem directivum."

To say the least, the opinion of these two eminent scholars is a probable one and may be followed in practical life.[27] For the silence of the Code is positive, not negative. In other words, the phrase "within a short time" had been officially interpreted to mean "within a month," and still the compiler of the Code used the vague expression "intra modicum tempus," in preference to the more precise phrase, "infra mensem." Consequently, the author of Canon 834 presumably omitted the latter phrase intentionally in order to deprive the old decree of its binding character and to relax the rigor of the antiquated regulation.[28]

The word "oblator" in Canon 834 refers primarily to the person who originally gave the offering; but the term includes a priest who transfers his stipends to some clerical friend of his, and also applies to the executor of a will. The person who thus hands over the offerings may

26 Blat, Liber II, pars. 1, p. 159.

26b Prümmer, "Manuale Theol. Mor.," Tom. III, p. 187.

27 Woywod, in the Homiletic and Pastoral Review, Vol. 21, p. 917.

28 Augustine, "A Commentary," Vol. I, p. 61; Cf. Praefatio in Codicem, p. xxxi.

be compared to the architect who sub-lets a contract. The builder may not change the specifications of his employer; but he may demand that the men to whom he sub-lets the contract finish their portion of the work within a time set by himself. So, too, may the priest or the executor who transfers stipends exact that the Masses be celebrated within an appointed time by the priest who accepts the intentions.

It is a mistake to object that the footnotes which are appended to Canon 834 in some editions of the Code refer to the interpretation contained in the decree "Ut debita." For those footnotes are of a purely private nature, and they have absolutely no authority of law. As Augustine says,[28] "Universal laws which oblige the whole Latin Church are, therefore, to be sought only in the Code, nor is it necessary to look for any other source, at least for juridical purposes. For Canon 6, n. 6, explicitly states that all other disciplinary laws thus far in force, if they are neither explicitly nor implicitly contained in this Code, must be held to have lost their obligatory force. This was precisely one of the chief objects set for the Codification Commission."

It seems, then, that canon law no longer obliges a priest to celebrate within a month any manual Mass except those which are requested for urgent intentions or at a specified time. He may defer for a reasonable time the celebration of such a Mass to suit his own convenience; but he must not put it off beyond the limit which is set by his own prudent conscience and by approved authors.[29] For instance, missionaries, monks, chaplains and student priests who receive large numbers of stipends from their clerical friends must be given more time to say the Masses than would be allowed to pastors.

Perhaps this is one reason why the Congregation of the Council refused to give its approval to the following scale:[30]

28 A Commentary, Vol. I, p. 61.
29 Blat, Liber III, pars. 1, p. 159.
30 Cf. S. C. C. decr. 27 Feb. 1905; A. S. S., Vol. XXXVII, p. 525.

10 Masses	one month
20 "	two months
40 "	three months
60 "	four months
80 "	five months
100 "	six months

Even if this scale had been approved, it would apply only to stipends which were received from the same individual. Less time is allowed for the celebration of many Masses requested by different people.[31] Cappello's rule is rigorous: He says that a priest who gets thirty stipends from thirty individuals must apply the thirty Masses within a month; whereas the priest who receives thirty stipends from three people may take three months to discharge the obligations.[32]

If the giver of a stipend tells the priest in these or equivalent words, "Father, you may say the Mass whenever you please," that Mass may be celebrated at any convenient time.[33] Innocent XII, in 1697, placed no restriction whatever upon the free will of the faithful who knowingly and willingly permitted a priest to defer their Mass for more than a year.[34] The same is true of the decree, "Ut debita," whose language is clearer than that of the Code. In that decree the Congregation of the Council taught that notwithstanding the prohibition of Masses which cannot be said within a year, the faithful might explicitly permit the postponement of their Masses

31 Ibid, ad. II.

32 Cf. Cappello, De Sacramentis, Vol. I, p. 548, n. 683—2°.

33 Cf. Canon 834, No. 3.

34 Cf. Innocentius XII, const. "Naper," 23 Dec. 1697, No. 15, ad 12; Cf. Fontes, Vol. I, p. 515. "Quamvis onera suscepta infra modicum tempus adimpleri nequeant, si tamen eleemosynam pro aliarum Missarum celebratione offerens id sciat, et consentiat, ut illae tunc demum celebrentur, cum susceptis oneribus satisfactum fuerit, Decretum non prohibere, quo minus eo casu eleemosyna accipiatur pro iisdem Missis iuxta Benefactoris consensum celebrandis."

or implicitly grant the celebrant a longer time by giving a comparatively large number of stipends.[35]

35 Cf. A. S. S., Vol. XXXVI, p. 673. 3° "Nemini licere tot Missas assumere quibus intra annum a die susceptae obligationis satisfacere probabiliter ipse nequeat; salva tamen semper contraria offerentium voluntate qui aut brevius tempus pro Missarum celebratione sive explicite sive implicite ob urgentem aliquam causam deposcant, aut longius tempus concedant, aut maiorem Missarum numerum sponte sua tribuant."

CHAPTER XVI

The One Year Limit or Canon 835

So intimately is Canon 835 connected with its predecessor that in the old law they formed two clauses of the same sentence.[1] The text of Canon 835 reads thus:[2] "Nemini licet tot Missarum onera per se celebrandarum recipere quibus intra annum satisfacere nequeat." It is incorrectly translated in this way:[3] "No one is allowed to receive more Masses than he himself can say within a year." Augustine's translation is more accurate:[4] "No one is allowed to receive more Masses to be celebrated by himself, than he can say within a year."

In the year 853, Pope Leo IV warned the clergy not to accept all the stipends which were offered to them.[5] The rest of this canon's history has been treated in the preceding chapter. Hence, the present chapter will deal only with the interpretation of the law.

The word "nemini," or "no one," does not include the Pope, for the Holy Father is not bound by the human laws which he or his predecessors have made.[6] On the other hand, the term "no one" is more precise than the expression "No priest"; for Canon 835 applies not only to ordinary priests, but also to Cardinals, Bishops, and even to laymen. It might happen, for instance, that some seminarian would collect a large number of stipends long before the time of his ordination. On the other hand, a

1 Cf. footnote (35) on p. 112 of this dissertation. Cf. S. C. C. decr. "Ut debita," 11 Maii, 1904, n. 3°.

2 Cf. Canon 835.

3 Cf. Woywod, The New Canon Law, p. 168, n. 678.

4 Cf. Augustine, A Commentary, Vol. IV, p. 199.

5 Cf. Mansi, Concilia, Vol. XIV, col. 494 and col. 1,005.

6 Cf. Canon 218.

student to whom a large sum of money is presented with a real obligation of saying a Mass later on for the donor, may keep the gift and say the Mass some day after his ordination. For the words "tot onera" indicate that Canon 835 was never meant to apply to such an exceptional case. Moreover, Canon 841 / 2 gives a wide scope to Canon 835; and the decree "Ut debita" added the phrase "salva diversa offerentium voluntate" to the law which is now contained in Canon 835. Hence, if people tell the priest expressly, "You may say these Masses at any time within the next two years," ecclesiastical law does not forbid the priest to accept those stipends and keep the intention for the time specified.[7b] The consent of the faithful, however, must be given freely, not under coercion.

The verb "licet" shows that this canon is not an invalidation or nullifying law, so that contracts which are entered into in violation of this regulation are valid, though illicit.[7] Consequently, a priest who has accumulated too many stipends may not refund the money, instead of saying the Masses, on the ground that an illegal contract is rescindible; for such a sacerdotal offender is obliged by ecclesiastical law, not to refund the superfluous stipends, but to transmit them to his Ordinary.[8]

Synonyms are not identical in meaning. At first the words "Tot Missarum onera" seem to mean the same as "stipendia Missarum"; but a moment's thought reveals the fact that the term "onera" is more precise because it is more general. For Canon 835 limits not the number of stipends alone, but rather the sum total of Masses which must be said from any title. For example, a curate may accept 364 stipends, whereas the pastor may not take more than 300 of these offerings.[9]

The phrase "per se" directly affects the person of Ordinaries and religious Superiors; indirectly it includes

7b Cf. A. S. S., Vol. XXXVI, p. 673.

7 Cf. Canon 11.

8 Cf. Canon 841, No. 1.

9 Cf. Canones 339, No. 1 and 466, No. 1. Cf. Blat, Liber II, De Personis, pp. 360-361.

also the stipends which they accept for Masses to be said by their subjects.[9a]

No priest may bind himself to say more Masses than he can celebrate within a year. But the Code does not forbid a pastor or curate to accept several hundred stipends for the purpose of sending them to other priests, provided that he has not agreed to offer up these Masses personally. In this way a priest can oblige all the people who want Masses said and at the same time he can help his fellow-priests who need the stipends.[10]

As regards the year within which all obligations must be discharged, the starting point is the date on which each stipend is received.[11] One person gives Father Jones a stipend on January 1, 1924, and another hands him ten offerings on December 6, 1924, both people leaving the time of their Masses to his convenience. In this hypothesis, the first Mass must be said on or before January 1, 1925; but the ten other Masses may be postponed until the ten days immediately preceding December 6, 1925. In the meanwhile, he may offer up three hundred Masses for other intentions, since there is no obligation of applying the Masses for the intentions in the order in which the corresponding stipends have been received.[12]

Moreover, if the time of celebration is expressly left to the priest and he should be hindered by sickness or suspension from saying the Mass within a year, he may deduct the days of his inability; count off 365 days on which he can say Mass, and then fulfill his obligation on the last of these days, which may come several years after he has accepted the stipends.[13] In other words, the year to which Canon 835 refers is a year of the so-called "tempus utile," as explained in Canon 34 / 2 and Canon

9a Cf. Blat, Liber III, pars. 1, De Sacramentis, p. 160.

10 Cf. The Homiletic and Pastoral Review, 1920-1921, Vol. 21, p. 918.

11 Cf. Canon 841, n. 2.

12 Cf. Canon 34, No. 3, N. 1° and n. 3°.

13 Cf. Cappello, De Sacramentis, Vol. I, p. 548, n. 3.

35.[14] This year's grace should be figured morally, not mathematically.[15]

For, after all, the primary object of Canon 835 is not to set the time within which any particular Mass must be celebrated, but to limit the number of obligations which priests may lawfully assume. It refers directly to the number of Masses, not to the time of their celebration. Its main purpose is to remove the cause for many petitions of reduction, to insure the application of a Mass for every stipend, and to check any avaricious tendency in connection with the Sacred Mysteries.

14 Cf. Blat, Liber III, pars. 1, p. 160; Cf. Canon 841, No. 2

15 Cf. Vermeersch, Epitome Iuris Canonici, Vol. II, p. 54, n. 106—4 ad. medium. "Quae omnia non mathematice sed moraliter sumenda sunt."

CHAPTER XVII

POSTERS
OR
CANON 836

When the National Shrine of the Immaculate Conception is completed, it will stand in the capital of the United States as a glorious monument to the faith of American Catholics and their devotion to the Mother of God. By a natural impulse of civic and religious pride, thousands of people who visit Washington will long to have a Mass for their intention celebrated in that magnificent shrine of America's Patroness. Occasionally it may become impossible to satisfy all these requests within the time prescribed by canon law.

To obviate the difficulty thus exemplified, the Code proposes a practical way of accepting those intentions without violating the obligations which those requests would otherwise impose. Canon 836 provides that a notice be posted in a conspicuous part of shrines, informing the faithful that the Masses which are there requested will be said either in the church itself, if convenient, or else in some other church.

"In ecclesiis in quibus ob fidelium peculiarem devotionem Missarum eleemosynae ita affluunt, ut omnes Missae, celebrari ibidem debito tempore nequeant, moneantur fideles, per tabellam in loco patenti et obvio positam, Missas oblatas celebratum iri vel ibidem cum commode poterit, vel alibi."

"In churches where, on account of the special devotion of the faithful, stipends for Masses are offered in such a number that it is impossible to say all of them in that church within the required time, the faithful should be notified by notices posted in a conspicuous place that the Holy Masses will be said either in that church when possible, or in other places." [1]

More than three hundred years ago the Congregation of the Council issued a decree which strongly resembles the present law.[2] "In posterum vero novas eleemosynas nullatenus recipi debere, nisi praevia expressa et clara monitione per sacristam (vel per tabellam dilucide descriptam et commodo loco affigendam) facienda offerentibus, non posse tam magnum numerum Missarum in eadem ecclesia, seu altari confestim celebrari, sed quod vel tractu temporis ibidem, cum commode fieri poterit, vel in alia ecclesia celebrabuntur."

The word "ecclesiis" in Canon 836 does not mean every church, as explained in Canon 1161; for as grammarians would say, the clause which modifies the noun in Canon 836 is restrictive, not explanatory.[3] In plain language, stipends which are offered in ordinary parish churches may be sent to other places without any further notice to the persons, because the giver of a stipend is ordinarily presumed to request nothing but the application of a Mass according to his intention.[4] But in any place where a special devotion of any kind exists, the mere fact that a stipend is offered in that shrine or sanctuary gives rise to the presumption that the circumstance of place is stipulated.

Augustine writes,[4b] "Evidently this rule applies only to churches where the faithful make their offerings personally, not to communities to which stipends are sent." The law, however, makes no such distinction; and to make this distinction frustrates the very purpose of the law. The people who visit a famous shrine do not always request Masses at the time of their visit: they send the

1 Woywod, The New Canon Law, p. 168, n. 679.

2 Cf. S. C. C., decr. Mediolanen, 8 mart., 1659; Cf. Benedict XIV, De Synodo Dioecesana, lib. XIII, cap. ult., n. 18; Cf. Link, Mess-Stipendien, p. 213.

3 For different view, vid. S. C. C., 9 Iulii, 1921; A. A. S., XIII, p. 504.

4 Arendt, "De Laesione," p. 2.

4b Cf. Augustine, A Commentary, Vol. IV, p. 200.

money later on, according as their devotion or their needs dictate.

If such visitors do not see any notice, they do not realize that thousands of other people are sending stipends to the same place. In their case, the presumption remains that they expect and require their Mass to be celebrated in the shrine itself.[5] On the contrary, if a notice has been posted in compliance with the wish of the church, then all petitioners are presumed to know the conditions that obtain in the shrine; and the clergy in charge of the church are free to send the stipends elsewhere.[6] But founded Masses committed to regulars without any further specification regarding the place of celebration may be said in any church of that Order;[7] and the same is true of manual Masses.[8] Perhaps this remark explains Augustine's commentary on Canon 836.

The sign or poster must really serve the purpose of the law. A poster which is hung in the belfry might be conspicuous (in loco patenti), but it would scarcely be legible (obvio positam). The notice should be such as to attract the attention of the faithful; it ought to be placed in the vestibule or on the bulletin board; and it must state plainly in the language of the people (not in Latin) that the Masses will be said in the church itself, if convenient, or else in some other place.

If the facts have thus been put before the faithful according to Canon 836, the people who give or send stipends without detailed instructions concerning the time or place at which their Masses must be said, are presumed to tacitly consent to the transfer or delay of their Masses. It seems, however, that most people who send their intentions to famous shrines subordinate time to place, and prefer to waive their rights of having the

5 Cf. Link, Mess-Stipendien, p. 213.

6 Cf. Blat, Liber III, pars. 1, p. 160 ad finem.

7 Cf. Zamboni, Collectio missa, No. 4, n. 18.

8 Cf. Link, Mess-Stipendien, p. 216.

Mass said within a short time (*e. g.*, a month) for the sake of having it said in the place of their devotion.[9]

If the petitioner indicated a particular place for some special but trifling reason, any reasonable cause justifies a priest in saying the Mass somewhere else; and if no such cause can be excogitated, the celebrant would at most commit a venial sin.[10] He who without reason celebrates a founded Mass once or twice a month in a place other than the one specified, commits a venial sin.[11] But per se it would be a mortal sin to change the place of celebration if that place was stipulated because of a special devotion to some saint; *e. g.*, to celebrate in another church a Mass for which the stipend had been sent to the National Shrine, with instructions that the Holy Sacrifice be offered up in the shrine and in honor of the Immaculate Conception.[12]

The Code itself seems to favor this view by putting this rule right after the laws on time, as if Canon 836 were an exception to the preceding canons and an extension of the time limit for Masses requested in such places.

9 Cf. Blat, Liber III, pars. i, De Sacramentis, p. 160. "Sic enim fideles eleemosynas offerentes consentiunt tacite in delationem vel in celebrationem extra ecclesiam, dum contrarium ipsos velle praesumendum esset."

10 Cf. De Lugo, n. 38, 40; Cf. Cappello, De Sacramentis, Vol. I, p. 552, n. 688.

11 Ibid; Cf. De Lugo, n. 36.

12 Cf. Cappello, De Sacramentis, Vol. I, p. 552, n. 688.

CHAPTER XVIII

DISTRIBUTION OF STIPENDS OR CANON 837

The administrators of shrines or other places of popular devotion often receive more requests for Masses than they can have celebrated in the shrine or other church. If they comply with Canon 836 by posting the prescribed notice in the vestibule, they may lawfully send away many of the intentions which have been received. Hence, upon the enactment concerning posters in popular churches, there follows logically a canon which begins a series of laws on a different but closely connected subject, viz.: the transfer of stipends.

Canon 837 consists of two co-ordinate clauses. The first of these asserts the right of every priest not only to accept stipends for himself, but also to transfer them to other priests of good repute; and the second clause modifies considerably the regulations about time which are laid down in the preceding canons. The text of Canon 837 reads,[1] "Qui Missas per alios celebrandas habet, eas quamprimum distribuat, firmo praescripto can. 841; sed tempus legitimum pro earundem celebratione incipit a die quo sacerdos celebraturus easdem receperit, nisi aliud constet." "He who has Masses which are to be said by others, should distribute them as soon as possible, observing Canon 841. The time prescribed by law for their application begins on the day on which the priest received them, unless the contrary is certain for other reasons."[2]

The decree "Ut debita" does not contain any regula-

1 Cf. Canon 837 in Codex Iuris Canonici.

2 Cf. Woywod, The New Canon Law, p. 168, n. 680.

tion which corresponds to Canon 837.[2a] In the year 1905, however, the Congregation of the Council was asked whether priests who received stipends from their Ordinary had to say the Masses within the prescribed time, beginning with the date on which the offerings had been received by the Bishop or Vicar General. The Congregation answered that the legal time within which the priest must say the Masses begins, not on the date when the stipends had been received by the Ordinary, but on the day when the actual celebrant receives the offerings. The Bishop, however, is told to see to it that intentions received from different sources be distributed among several priests.[3] "Obligationem incipere a die quo sacerdotes Missas celebrandas ab Ordinario recipiunt." [3]

The Latin pronoun "qui" extends the canon to all Christians who are obliged to dispose of Mass stipends. Canon 844 / 1 makes the Ordinary of the place and religious Superiors official trustees or custodians of supernumerary stipends.[4] In some religious communities the Superior delegates this function to a priest, who is called the "intentionarius" and whose official duty it is to distribute the Mass intentions among the priests of his Order or Congregation.[5] Even the ordinary secular priest in a parish often receives more intentions for Masses than he can licitly keep for himself.[6]

Laymen, too, are bound by this canon. For instance, the executor of a will ought to comply with the law of the Church by having those Masses celebrated as soon as possible, which the legator has requested in his last will.[6b] Here the civil law comes into play. In the case of Kehoe *vs.* Kehoe, Judge Tuley held, in 1883, that the law of Illinois does not consider Mass stipends to be bequests

2a Cf. S. C. C., decr. "Ut debita," 11 Maii, 1904, n. 4; Cf. A. S. S., Vol. XXXVI, pp. 672-674.

3 Cf. S. C. C. decr. 27 Feb. 1905, ad 3; Cf. A. S. S., Vol. XXXVII, p. 526; Cf. Hilling, Die Mess-Stipendien und Stolgebühren, p. 30.

4 Cf. Canon 844, No. 1.

5 Cf. Augustine, A Commentary, Vol. IV, p. 201.

6 Cf. Blat, Liber III, pars. 1, p. 161.

6b Cf. Vermeersch, Epitome, Vol. II, p. 55, n. 8.

for superstitious uses.[7] But in New York, in the case of Holland *vs.* Alcock, the Court of Appeals held that a trust for Masses was void because the intended beneficiary (*i. e.*, the soul for whom the Masses were to be said) was not a living person whose rights the law could take cognizance of and enforce.[8]

The civil law of Pennsylvania practically ignores the priest and considers the executor alone. The executor, not the priest, is responsible for the saying of the Masses. Money for Masses should not be left to the Archbishop of Philadelphia as a corporation sole, but to Archbishop Dougherty as private individual, who bears the title of Archbishop or Cardinal, just as a pastor is called Father Smith or Doctor Jones.

A person who wishes to have Masses said for himself after death should not make the celebration of those Masses a necessary condition (conditio sine qua non) of the bequest. In other words, he ought to use a formula like this, "I will and bequeath to the Reverend John Smith, the present curate of St. Mary's Church in Refound Creek, the sum of five hundred dollars; and I ask, but in no way oblige, him to say one hundred Low Masses for me at intervals convenient to himself and extending over a period of several years."

Canon 837 urges, but does not command, a priest to dispose of superfluous stipends "as soon as possible." There is no reason for any explanation of the "quamprimum," because the first clause of Canon 837 states a counsel, not a command. The command is given in Canon 841, which expressly permits every priest to keep ordinary manual stipends for a whole year before sending them away.

More difficulty is experienced by the jurists who attempt to explain the second part of the present canon.[10] The legal time (tempus legitimum) to which Canon 837

7 Cf. Dillon, Bequests for Masses, p. 29.

8 Cf. Dillon, Bequests for Masses, p. 33.

10 Cf. Vermeersch-Creusen, Epitome, Vol. II, p. 55, n. 7.

refers is to be understood in the sense of Canon 834: if the giver of the stipend expressly prescribes the time of the Mass, the Holy Sacrifice must be offered at that time; if not, then Masses for urgent intentions must be said as soon as possible, and other Masses within a comparatively short time.

But suppose that Father B receives a stipend for an ordinary intention on June 1st. On June 29th he sends that stipend to Father C and tells him that it was received on June 1st. If Father C accepts the stipend, must he say the Mass within a few days, or may he put it off for another month, *i. e.*, until July 29th or thereabouts? That is the question to be considered.[11]

Vermeersch contends that a Superior or other priest who has undertaken to say the Mass can not licitly prolong the legal time by holding the stipend until the period prescribed in the Code has almost expired. In other words, this eminent canonist considers Father C obliged to say the Mass on or about July 1st, although he has received the stipend only two or three days before that date.[12]

Cappello [13] and Woywod seem to favor the view that the actual celebrant of the Mass is entitled to the period of grace ordained in Canon 834.[14] Blat [15] calls attention to the fact that the time does not begin on the date when the intentions or Masses (not the stipends) are *sent* by the first priest, but it commences on the day when the intentions are *received* by the celebrant.

Before the Code, the Congregation of the Council answered expressly that the priests' obligation begins on the day when they receive the intentions from the Ordinary.[16] Although this obsolete decree is now only

11 Cf. Augustine, A Commentary, Vol, IV, p. 201.

12 Cf. Vermeersch-Creusen, Epitome, Vol. II, p. 55, n. 8.

13 Cf. Cappello, De Sacramentis, Vol. I, p. 548, n. 683-3.

14 Cf. Woywod in Homiletic and Pastoral Review, 1920-1921, Vol. 21, p. 919.

15 Cf. Blat, Liber III, pars. 1, p. 161.

16 Cf. S. C. C., 27 Feb. 1905; A. S. S., Vol. XXXVII, p. 525. Cf. Hilling, Die Mess-Stipendien u. Stolgebühren, p. 30. Ad. III: "Affirmative, idest obligationem incipere a die quo sacerdotes Missas celebrandas ab Ordinario recipiunt."

a directive norm, still it elucidates the mind of the legislator.[17]

The last clause "nisi aliud constet" is added because the Code always makes provision for special stipulation, and because no such stipulation is cancelled by the transference of a stipend. Hence, if a day is specified for an anniversary Mass, or if a Mass for a proximate operation is requested, the celebrant who receives the stipend is bound to observe the circumstance of time, just as the first priest who transmitted the offering would have been bound to do so.[17b]

No Bishop should send a large number (*e. g.*, a hundred) of Masses at a time to any priest. If the Ordinary wishes to favor an individual, he can arrange with him to send a few (*e. g.*, twenty) intentions every month.

In some parishes the pastors announce as high as six daily Masses, "These Masses will be said in this church, or in St. N's Church." Such a pastor may simply tell the curate in the other parish: "Every day say your Mass according to my intention; and at the end of each month I shall send you my check for the proper amount." [18] This arrangement is not the ideal way of doing things, for the celebrant ought to know a little more about the intention for which his Mass is being applied.[19] Nevertheless, the agreement could be tolerated, because it is sufficient for priests to say their Mass according to the intention of the priest or Bishop who sent them the stipend, and they need not care about the original intention of him who first made the offering.[20]

17 Cf. Canon 6, n. 2. "Canones qui ius vetus exintegro referunt, exveteris iuris auctoritate, atque ideo ep receptis apud probatos auctores interpretationibus, sunt aestimandi."; Cf. Blat, Liber III, pars. 1, p. 161: "Ut norma praxis solum directiva iuvat referre quaedam praecedentia Decreta."

17b Cf. Cappello, De Sacramentis, Vol. I, p, 567, n. 706.

18 Cf. Hilling, Die Mess-Stipendien u. Stolgebühren, p. 30 ad finem.

19 Cf. S. C. C., 27 Feb., 1905 ad. V; A. S. S., Vol. XXXVII, p. 526: "Sufficere ut sacerdotes celebrent iuxta mentem Ordinarii; qui tamen intentionem pro singulis offerentibus efformare debet iuxta regulas a probatis theologiae moralis auctoribus traditas. Melius tamen esse si patefiant sacerdotibus intentiones praescriptae."

20 Cf. Link, Mess-Stipendien, p. 216.

Nay, a priest who is ignorant of the giver's intention and says the Mass simply "ad intentionem dantis," fulfills his obligation, even though he should celebrate a Requiem Mass for a soldier's safe return.[21] But suppose a priest receives ten stipends and is told to say ten Masses "ad intentionem dantis." He does not know whether the ten intentions are the same, or whether there are ten distinct intentions of so many different people. He may, if he wish, offer up the ten Masses "for the intentions of the givers," on the principle that ten times one-tenth of a Mass's fruit equal the fruit of one Mass.[22] One can hardly agree, however, with a certain writer who recommends this form because he thinks that the usual formula "ad intentionem dantis" is not sufficiently specific.[23]

21 Cf. S. C. C., 29 Nov. 1856; Cf. Link, Mess-Stipendien, p. 216, n. 4.

22 Cf. Link, p. 217.

23 Cf. Ecclesiastical Review, Vol. 42, p. 745.

CHAPTER XIX

THE CONSIGNEE OF STIPENDS
OR
CANON 838

A priest who is bound by canon law to send stipends to his confreres is not entirely free to commit the celebration of the Masses to any other priest of his own choosing. Canon 838 enumerates the classes of priests to whom such superfluous stipends may be transferred. It reads:[1] "Qui habent Missarum numerum de quibus sibi liceat libere disponere, possunt eas tribuere sacerdotibus sibi acceptis, dummodo probe sibi constet eos esse omni exceptione maiores vel testimonio proprii Ordinarii commendatos."

"He who has a number of Masses which he is allowed to give to others, may distribute them among priests of his choice, provided he knows they are absolutely trustworthy or are recommended by the testimony of their Ordinary."[2]

The old law required of Ordinaries that they be acquainted personally with the extra-diocesan priests to whom they send superfluous stipends directly,[3] and another decree applied the same ruling to priests who send such offerings to their sacerdotal confreres.[4] The present law modifies the rigor of these two decrees, which form

1 Cf. Canon 838, C. I. C.

2 Cf. Woywod, The New Canon Law, p. 169, n. 681.

3 Cf. S. C. C., decr. "Vigilanti," 25 Maii, 1893; A. S. S., Vol. XXVI, p. 56.

4 Cf. S. C. C., decr. "Ut debita," 11 Maii, 1904, n. 5; A. S. S., Vol. XXXVI, p. 673. "Qui exuberantem Missaram numerum habent, de quibus sibi liceat libere disponere (quin fundatorum vel oblatorum voluntati quoad tempus et locum celebrationis Missarum detrahatur), posse eas tribuere praeterquam proprio Ordinario aut S. Sedi, sacerdotibus quoque sibi benevisis, dummodo certe ac personaliter sibi notis et omni exceptione maioribus."

its basis. The Code requires, not personal acquaintance, but mere certainty that Masses will be said.

A priest may transfer his overplus of offerings for Masses to any of the following physical or moral persons:

1. The Holy See (Propaganda or Congregation of the Council);[6]
2. The Apostolic Delegate;[7]
3. The priest's Ordinary (Bishop, Vicar General, Chancellor);[8]
4. Priests whose own Ordinary vouches for their integrity (*e. g.*, per "Celebret");[9]
5. Any good priest with whom the sacerdotal giver of the stipend is personally acquainted;[10]
6. Other priests whose integrity is known from other sources (*e. g.*, the Superior of Religious);[11]

Canon 838 contains the words "omni exceptione maiores." These words constitute a phrase which is borrowed from the ecclesiastical court room, and which means that the people in question are above suspicion.[11a]

Cappello teaches that a Bishop can forbid priests to send their stipends wherever they please.[12] Cappello's teaching is erroneous.[13] There even exists a very plain decree to the contrary. Some one asked whether a provincial law forbidding priests to send stipends out of the diocese could be sustained as "praeter legem" after the promulgation of the Code of Canon Law. The answer

6 S. C. C., decr. "Ut debita," n. 6.

7 Cf. Canon 267/2.

8 Cf. Hilling, "Mess-Stipendien u. Stolgebühren," p. 11.

9 Cf. A. S. S., Vol. XIII, p. 228.

10 Cf. Bargilliat, "Les Honoraires de Messes," p. 33/II, n. 1 ad finem.

11 Cf. Blat, Liber III, pars. 1, p. 163.

11a Cf. Reiffenstuel, Ius Canonicum, II, 20, 10-11. "Omni exceptione maiores sunt iidem qui optimi, seu in quos suspicio cadere nequit. Hoc proprie dicitur de teste qui egregie idoneus est."

12 Cf. Cappello, De Sacramentis, Vol. I, p. 569, n. 706 ad fin.

13 Cf. S. C. C., decr. 19 Feb., 1921; A. A. S., Vol. XIII, p. 228-230.

was "No." [14] The reason underlying this response is that no Bishop can lawfully go contrary to papal law. Hence, such a prescription on the part of a Bishop is contrary to Canon 838, which clearly grants to all priests the fullest liberty of sending money for Masses to other Latin priests of good repute.

The decree "Complures" provides: that stipends may be sent to priests of an Oriental Rite through the Apostolic Delegate in the Oriental country, but they may not be sent to lay distributors in the East, nor to Oriental priests, nor even to a titular Bishop in the Orient.[15] An American priest, for instance, may send stipends to Ordinaries residing in the East; but such a priest must inform the Oriental Apostolic Delegate how many stipends have been sent and to whom they were sent.[16]

The phrase "in the Orient" means those sections of Eastern Europe and Western Asia in which the Oriental rites predominate. This matter is a question of rite, not of geography, so that, as regards Canon 838, Egypt is an Oriental country, whereas China and the Philippine Islands do not belong to the Orient.

Some authorities teach that the decree "Complures" seems to remain in force in virtue of the first canon, because the Code does not abrogate the decrees which were issued primarily for the Oriental Church.[16] Others contend that this decree has lost the force of law, because it applies to priests of the Latin rite directly and only indirectly affects the Oriental clergy.

Theoretically, both opinions are probable. In practice, however, a doubtful law is not binding; the decree is at most only a doubtful one; consequently, a priest may with good conscience send stipends directly to Oriental friends or acquaintances.[16a]

14 Cf. Vermeersch, Epitome, Vol. II, p. 56, n. 1.

15 Cf. S. C. de prop. Fid., 15 Iulii, 1908; A. S. S., Vol. XII, p. 460.

16 Cf. Blat, Liber III, pars. 1, p. 164.

16a Cf. Canon 6, n. 6.

As far as canon law is concerned, he may give manual stipends to a Greek Ruthenian priest in America, for giving stipends is not the same as sending or transmitting them.

CHAPTER XX

DURATION OF THE TRANSFERRER'S OBLIGATIONS
OR
CANON 839

One the principle that to have something done by another is equivalent to doing it one's self, business men are permitted to sub-let their contracts; but they are held responsible for the workmanship of their subordinates. In a similar manner canon law permits a priest to transfer his obligation of saying a Mass in return for a stipend; but it binds him to see to it that the contract is faithfully fulfilled by his agent. Canon 839 obliges him to select priests of unimpeachable integrity to celebrate his overplus of Masses. Canon 839 further safeguards the right of him who gives a stipend by holding the recipient of that offering responsible for the celebration of the Mass until he learns for sure that some other reliable priest has agreed to say the Mass in his stead.

The text of Canon 839 reads: "Qui Missas a fidelibus receptas aut quoquo modo suae fidei commissas aliis celebrandas tradiderint, obligatione tenentur usque dum acceptatae ab eisdem obligationis et recepti stipendii testimonium obtinuerint." A translation of this canon says, "He who has given to other priests Masses which he received from the faithful, or which are in any way entrusted to him, is held to their obligation until he received notice that the stipends were received by the priest and that he has accepted to say the Masses." [1]

The wording of the present canon resembles that of its source, viz.: the decree "Ut debita," which reads in part as follows: "Qui vero Missas a fidelibus susceptas, aut utcumque suae fidei commissas, aliis celebrandas tradiderint, obligatione teneri usque dum peractae cele-

1 Cf. Woywod, The New Canon Law, p. 169, n. 682.

brationis fidem non sint assequuti."[2] The meaning of the new law, however, differs considerably from that of the old legislation.

In the old law, a priest could relieve himself of all further obligation by sending the stipends to his own Ordinary or to the Holy See.[3] The Code contains no such provision; and therefore this obsolete paragraph of an antiquated decree no longer has the force of law.[4]

Secondly, the priest who first received a stipend was held responsible by the old law for the corresponding Mass until he had been informed that the second priest had not only agreed to say the Mass in his stead, but had already offered up the Holy Sacrifice for the prescribed intention.[5] The Code is more lenient. At present, if a second priest of good repute assumes the obligation, the first priest is released from further responsibility, even before the Mass is actually celebrated.

Manual stipends are so called because they are usually given from the hands of the faithful into the hands of the celebrant. Yet there are many other ways in which the application of a Mass in return for a stipend may be entrusted to a priest. He may receive a number of such offerings as a bequest. He may be charged as the executor of a will to have a number of Masses celebrated. As the administrator of a pious foundation, he may be obliged to see to it that the founded Masses are said regularly. If he be a Bishop, Vicar General or Chancellor, it may be his duty to distribute the overplus of stipends which the diocesan priests have sent to him in compliance with Canon 841.[6]

2 Cf. S. C. C., decr. "Ut debita, 11 Maii, 1904, n. 6; A. S. S., XXXVI, 674.

3 Ibid, n. 6. "Qui Missas cum sua eleemosyna proprio Ordinario aut S. Sedi tradiderint ab omni obligatione coram Deo et Ecclesia relevari."

4 Cr. Canon 6, n. 6; Cf. Blat, Liber III, pars. I, p. 164, ad finem. Cf. Blat, Liber III, pars. 1, p. 164, ad finem; Cf. Canon 6, n. 6. "Si qua ex ceteris disciplinaribus legibus quae usque adhuc viguerunt, nec explicite nec implicite in Codice contineatur, ea vim omnem amisisse dicenda est, nisi in probatis liturgicis libris reperiatur, aut lex sit iuris divini sive positivi sive naturalis."

5 Cf. S. C. C., decr. "Ut debita," 11 Maii, 1904, n. 6; Cf. p. 249.

6 Cf. Blat, Liber III, pars. 1, p. 164 ad finem.

Canon 839 uses the word "obligation" (obligatione) to indicate that the burden which rests upon the transferrer of stipends is a twofold obligation, not only to have the Mass celebrated for the giver of the stipend, but also to remunerate the celebrant of the Mass by delivering to him the proper offering for that Mass. It is not enough to *send* the stipend; it must be actually *delivered* to the second priest, he must accept it, and he must inform the sender that he has received the money and assumes the obligation of saying the Mass.[7] Hence, if the first stipend is lost, even though it happen through no fault of the sender or of anybody else, the first priest at his own expense must deliver another stipend to the celebrant or second priest who assumes the obligation.[8]

Sometimes the intentions and the stipends are given separately: a priest is asked to say a number of Masses, and the money is sent to him later. Even though such intentions have been accepted and the Masses said, the priest who sends the stipends, not the one who celebrates the Mass, is the loser if the money is lost in the mail.[9]

In Canon 839, the word "testimonium" does not mean proof in the legal sense of the term. Nor does the Code demand an authentic notice from the priest to whom the money is sent and the intentions committed. Any information which makes the sender sure that the stipends and the intentions have been accepted releases him from all further responsibility.[10]

No document is required if the Masses are transferred personally from one priest to another; *e. g.*, from pastor to curate.[11] If a trustworthy messenger reports that he has delivered the stipends to a priest who accepted them, the sender need not demand any other proof. Hence, it is not necessary to send the letter by regis-

7 Cf. Canon 839.

8 Cf. Cappello, De Sacramentis, Vol. I, p. 568, n. 707, In.

9 Cf. S. C. C., decr. "Ut debita," 11 Maii, 1904, n. 6.

10 Cf. Cappello, De Sacramentis, Vol. I, p. 568, n. 707. Cf. Blat, Liber III, pars. 1, p. 165.

11 Cf. Bargilliat, "Les Honoraires de Messes," p. 36, c.

tered mail.[12] The return receipt for a registered letter, which was marked "Deliver to addressee only," leaves hardly any room for doubt that the stipends and intentions have reached their destination and have been accepted by the priest to whom they were sent. Nevertheless, if that priest proves that his signature was forged, the sender would still be responsible for the Masses. The same is true of a letter purporting to come from such a priest.

If the stipends are sent out of the United States, a bank draft is the safest means of transmitting the money.

Throughout this chapter the word "priest" has been used. But the same remarks apply to a Bishop who sends stipends to another Bishop.[14] Finally, if an indorsed check, a receipt for registered mail, or a personal letter is ordinarily sufficient to release a priest from further concern about transferred stipends, a fortiori he is released by an official notice that the Bishop or religious Superior has received and accepted the Mass intentions.[15]

12 Cf. Cappello, De Sacramentis, Vol. I, p. 568, n. 707.

13 Cf. Canon 839.

14 Cf. A. S. S., Vol. XXXVII, p. 527.

15 Cf. S. C. C., Decr. "Ut debita," 11 Maii, 1904, n. 6; Cf. Blat, Liber III, pars. 1, p. 163, b.

CHAPTER XXI

The Indivisibility of Manual Stipends or Canon 840

Canon 839 says that the actual celebrant of a Mass is entitled to the stipend thereof. The next canon adds that the actual celebrant of a Mass is entitled to the *whole* stipend if it be a manual one, but to the diocesan tax only if the offering be made for a quasimanual Mass. The text is clear:

"Qui Missarum stipes manuales ad alios transmittit, debet acceptas integre transmittere, nisi aut oblator expresse permittat aliquid retinere, aut certo constet excessum supra taxam dioecesanam datum fuisse intuitu personae.

"In Missis ad instar manualium, nisi obstet mens fundatoris, legitime retinetur excessus et satis est remittere solam eleemosynam manualem dioecesis in qua Missa celebrantur, si pinguis eleemosyna locum pro parte teneat dotis beneficii aut causae piae."

This canon means that:

"He who transmits manual stipends to others must send away the stipends as he received them, and can not retain part of larger stipends, unless the giver expressly permits this, or it is certain that what was offered above the usual stipend was given *intuitu personae,* that is to say, for special personal reasons.

"In Masses *ad instar manualium* (Cf. Canon 826), unless the intention of the founder is otherwise, the excess of the ordinary stipend may be retained if the larger stipend takes the place of a partial endowment of the benefice or pious institution, and it is sufficient to send the manual stipend customary in the place where the Masses are to be said." [1]

1 Woywod, "The New Canon Law," p. 169, n. 683.

A whole book has been written about one phase of the subject matter contained in Canon 840.[2] Evidently, the present chapter can contain little more than a summary of that scholastic thesis. These pages, moreover, will treat, not so much about the theological aspect of the subject as did that scholarly essay, but rather concerning the history and juridical interpretation of Canon 840.

Francis Suarez, in the beginning of the seventeenth century, was the first theologian to propose the doctrine that it is not intrinsically unjust or contrary to the *natural* law for a pastor to accept an offering for a Mass and then have the Mass said by another priest, to whom he gives only a part of the original stipend.[3]

On the contrary, Cardinal De Lugo,[5] the Prince of Moralists; Diana,[6] the Prince of Laxists; and Reiffenstuel,[7] a reputable canonist, all agree with a host of other authorities[8] that *per se* the priest who accepts an offering but transfers the celebration of the Mass to another priest has no right even under the natural law to keep any part of the formal stipend.[9]

People who give money for Masses usually do so for the sole purpose of having those Masses celebrated and applied according to the givers' intentions. Therefore, the whole amount of the offering is generally intended for the sustenance of the priest who says the Mass. Con-

2 Cf. Arendt, "De Laesione Iustitiae commutativae in Missae Manualis Stipendio Alteri Celebranti Diminuto," Prati, 1914.

3 Cf. Suarez, "De Missae Sacrificio," Disp. 86, Sect. III, n. 7. "Ego vero censeo intrinsece non esse hoc contra iustitiam. . . Ratio autem a priori est, quia parochus vel sacerdos, qui primo accipit stipendium, statim acquirit dominium illius sub obligatione dicendi Missam alteri, quam potest per se vel per alium implere."

4 Cf. Arendt, "De Laesione," p. 72 and p. 144.

5 Cf. De Lugo, "De Eucharistia," Disp. XXI, sect. II, n. 26 and n. 32; Cf. Arendt, "De Laesione," p. 98-100.

6 Cf. Diana, Theol. Mor., Tom II, Tract. I, Resol. 25; Cf. Arendt, "De Laesione," pp. 102-105.

7 Cf. Reiffenstuel, "Theologea Moralis," 1st ed., Tract. XIV, Dis. V., n. 95; Cf. Arendt, "De Laesione," p. 114.

8 Cf. Sanchez Laymann, Aversa, Pasqualigo, Pignatelli, etc., apud Arendt, "De Laesione," p. 95-113.

9 Cf. Arendt, "De Laesione," p. 144.

sequently, the priest who accepts a manual stipend and then asks another priest to apply the Mass is obliged by the natural law to give the whole formal stipend to the actual celebrant. Failure to do so constitutes a mortal sin against commutative justice and binds the delinquent to make restitution to the priest who has said the Mass.[10] This is the gist of Arendt's dissertation on "The Violation of Commutative Justice Through the Diminution of the Stipend for a Transferred Manual Mass." [11]

Nevertheless, the natural law leaves some room for doubt.[11b] Concerning canon law, there can be no doubt. In 1625, Pope Urban VIII [12] forbade priests to keep a part of the stipend for an intention which they had transferred to a fellow-priest. In 1665, Alexander VII condemned the opposite doctrine as erroneous.[13] In 1697, Innocent XII reiterated the law verbatim, and added that the whole stipend must absolutely go to the celebrant, even if that offering exceeded the usual stipend.[14]

Benedict XIV excommunicated the layman and suspended the cleric who dared to collect stipends with the intention of having the Masses celebrated at a lower rate and keeping the difference thus accruing.[15] A century later the Congregation of the Council implicitly forbade priests to expend on good works the money which they had subtracted from stipends for Masses which other priests would willingly celebrate for such reduced offerings.[16] Pius IX [17] retained in the constitution "Apostolicae Sedis" the excommunication which Benedict XIV

10 Cf. S. C. C., 23 Aug. 1664, Link, p. 230, a.

11 Cf. Arendt, "De Laesione," p. 42.

11b Cf. Arendt, "De Laesione," p. 1.

12 Cf. S. C. C., decr. 21 Iunii, 1625/5; Cf. Link, p. 221.

13 Cf. Fontes, Vol. I, p. 510/6.

14 Cf. Denzinger-Bannwart, Euchiridion, p. 345, n. 1109.

15 Cf. Benedictus XIV, encycl. "Quanta cura," 30 Iun. 1741/5; Cf. Fontes, I, pp. 682 and 683.

16 S. C. C., decr. 19 Ian. 1689; Cf. Link, p. 222, b.

17 Cf. Pius IX, Const. "Apostolicae Sedis," 12 Oct., 1869/11, n. 12.

had fulminated against profiteering collectors of stipends; and he even extended the censure to clerics.[18]

The pronoun "qui" at the beginning of Canon 840 makes it evident that this law applies to laymen as well as to clerics. This statement is confirmed by Canon 2324, which permits the Bishop to suspend a priest and to excommunicate a layman who violates Canon 840 / 1.[21] The Code thus changes the former penalties from censures "latae sententiae" into penalties "ferendae sententiae." In other words, the suspension or excommunication is no longer incurred "ipso facto": it is now incumbent upon the Ordinary to punish infractions of this law.[18]

The decree "Ut debita" stated that the offering for Masses could never be separated from the celebration of those Masses, nor diminished, nor changed into other goods, nor used in part for the ornamentation of churches.[19]

A recent decree forbids priests to keep a part of those stipends which are offered for "Announced Masses" that are celebrated by other priests.[20] It is true that "Announced Masses" confer an extrinsic title to something more than the diocesan fee for an ordinary Mass, nevertheless, the "Announced Mass" confers this extrinsic title, not upon the pastor who makes the announcement, but upon the curate who celebrates the Mass. The burden of saying the Mass, or of having it said on the day announced, rests, not upon the announcer, but on the celebrant or other priest who accepts the stipend. Hence, it is absolutely forbidden to give the celebrant of an "Announced Mass" the usual stipend and to keep the rest of the offering for merely announcing the Mass.[21] For Canon 840 says explicitly that he who sends manual stipends to other people ought to send the entire offer-

18 Cf. Leech, "A Comparative Study," p. 67.

19 Cf. S. C. C., decr., "Ut debita," 11 Maii, 1904/9 and n. 11. Cf. A. S. S., Vol. XXXVI, p. 675.

20 Cf. S. C. C., decr., 25 Feb. 1905; A. S. S., Vol. XXXVIII, p. 15.

21 Cf. Hilling, Die Mess-Stipendien und Stolgebühren, pp. 22-23.

ing which he himself has received; "debet acceptas *integre* transmittere." [22]

Although the law prescribes that the whole stipend be sent to the celebrant of the Mass, still the sender may lawfully deduct therefrom all the expenses of transmission, such as postage and registration.[22a]

The Code itself mentions two exceptions to its own rule: the sender may keep part of the stipend if the receiver permits him to do so, or if it is certain that a portion of the offering was given for purely personal reasons. Thus, if a stranger officiates at the wedding or the funeral of a relative, he generally foregoes his right to the stipend by custom or from gratitude; and the pastor may usually keep the entire fee for the wedding or funeral, because the celebration of the Mass by the visiting priest was permitted, not "committed," by the pastor.[22b]

The sacerdotal relative may indeed insist upon his rights and demand a stipend for the Nuptial Mass. In that case, he is entitled to the diocesan stipend of one dollar for a Low Mass or five dolars for High Mass. The rest of the marriage fee may be kept by the pastor and curates of the parish, because it has been given to them partly as a stole fee.[22c]

If a person bequeaths to a priest a sum of money for a *specified* number of Masses, "I will and bequeath to Father Doe a thousand dollars for a *hundred* Masses to be said for the repose of my soul," that priest may have some or all of those Masses said by other priests, to whom he need give only the usual fee.[23] In other words, if the first priest is the beneficiary of a will, he may keep the surplus; but if he is merely the executor, he must give the actual celebrant the entire stipend pre-

22 Cf. Canon 840/1.

22a Cf. Gasparri, "De Eucharistia," Vol. I, p. 445, n. 609.

22b Cf. De Lugo, "De Sacramento Eucharistia," Disp. XXI, n. 32; Cf. Gasparri, "De Eucharistia," Vol. I, p. 438, n. 599, ad finem.

22c Cf. S. C. C., decr. 25 Iulii, 1874, apud Gasparri, "De Eucharistia," Vol. I, p. 441, n. 603.

23 Cf. Gasparri, "De Eucharistia," Vol. I, p. 443, n. 605.

scribed in the will for the Masses which the executor himself does not celebrate or apply.[24]

Moreover, the priest may keep the excess above the diocesan offering if the giver of that stipend expressly stated that the surplus was given for some personal reason, *e. g.*, because of the priest's rank (monsignor), position (pastor), relationship (nephew). A pastor, however, is not to presume rashly that every parishioner who offers him money for Masses intends to give the surplus to him for personal reasons, rather than to the curate for saying the Mass.[25]

Since the Code, the Holy See was asked whether publishers might lawfully send American magazines to European priests who could not afford to pay the subscription, but who would gladly say Masses for the intention of the publishers. In this case, the publishers were not soliciting or collecting stipends; rather, it was the priests who asked for the magazines. The unpublished answer was, "Non expedire," which means that the Holy See does not absolutely condemn the practice, but certainly does not approve of it.

It is unlawful for a priest to tell the celebrant, "I shall give you two dollars for saying your Mass today according to my intention, on condition that you let me keep the remainder of the stipend." [26] But if the celebrant of his own accord foregoes a part or the whole of an offering, he is simply giving up his right; and that is nobody's concern except his own.[27] Thus European priests often write to their American friends, "I shall gladly say your dollar Masses for seventy-five cents." Such a transaction is tolerable but not commendable. Benedict XIV seems to forbid this; but really he denounces it only when the consent of the celebrant is compulsory.

Canon 840 does not mention founded Masses, because

24 Cf. Gasparri, "De Eucharistia," Vol. I, p. 444, n. 605.

25 Ibid, n. 606.

26 Collectanea, n. 1200.

27 Cf. Gasparri, "De Eucharistia," Vol. I, p. 447, n. 611.

these are regulated by other principles.[28] When on occasion a founded Mass can not be celebrated by the proper priest (*e. g.*, the beneficiary), he may engage a substitute to say the Mass for him. This Mass is known as a quasi-manual Mass.[29] The second section of Canon 840 lays down the law that the substitute who says the quasi-manual Mass is generally entitled to the diocesan stipend of the place where that Mass is celebrated, but not to any excess above that amount.

This regulation may be traced back through the decree "Ut debita" to the constitution "Nuper" of Innocent XII.[31] The present law, however, differs from the former discipline in an important respect: the decree "Ut debita" provided that the stipend for a quasi-manual Mass should be the same as the manual stipend of the place where the benefice was erected;[32] whereas the Code prescribes that the celebrant of a quasi-manual Mass be given the usual stipend of the place where he says the Mass.[33] For example, if an American pastor on a pilgrimage to Rome cannot offer up his "Missa Pro Populo," he may engage an Italian priest to say that Mass in his stead. Before the Code, the pastor would have been obliged to give the Italian priest the American stipend of one dollar; but since the Code, he has to give that celebrant only the Italian stipend of five lires, or about 25 cents. In Canon 840 / 2 the Code mentions three exceptions to its own rule. First, a pastor need give only a manual stipend to the curate for saying the Missa Pro

28 Cf. Arendt, "De Laesione," p. 2; Cf. S. C. C., decr. "Ut debita," 11 Maii, 1904, n. 15; Cf. Arendt, "De Laesione," p. 2.

29 Cf Canon 826/2.

31 Cf. Innocentius XII, const. "Nuper," 23 Dec. 1697/15, ad 7, 8; Fontes, Vol. I, p. 515; Cf. S. C. C., decr. 23 Nov. 1697, ad 7, 8; Cf. Fontes, Vol. I, p. 515.

32 Cf. A. S. S., Vol. XXXVI, p. 676; Cf. S. C. C., decr. "Ut debita," 11 Maii, 1904/15. "Denique quod spectat Missas beneficiis adnexas, quoties aliis sacerdotibus celebrandae traduntur, Eminentissimi Patres declarant ac statuunt, eleemosynam non aliam esse debere quam synodalem loci in quo beneficia erecta sunt."

33 Cf. Canon 840/2. "Satis est remittere solam elemosynam manualem dioecesis in qua Missa celebratur."

Populo, because the income of the benefice is intended to be the salary for the pastor's whole sustenance, not merely to be the stipends for the Masses which he must say for his parishioners.[34] Second, when a person bequeaths a sum of money to a hospital with the obligation of having one or more Masses said annually, the hospital may give the celebrant the ordinary stipend and lawfully keep the excess; for that surplus is intended for the maintenance of the hopital, not for the support of the celebrant.[35] Third, someone, especially an American Catholic, may bequeath or endow a "founded" Mass in the wide sense of the term, viz., a perpetual Mass which has not been assigned by the founder to any particular priest or church. In this case, the Bishop may assign the Masses to some priest; but if that priest is hindered from saying one or more of those Masses, he must give his substitute the whole offering for that Mass (not merely the diocesan stipend for a manual Mass), because in this instance the founder is presumed to favor the celebrant alone.[36]

34 Cf. Canon 840/2, "Legitime retinetur excessus . . . si pinguis eleemosyna locum pro parte teneat dotis beneficii."

35 Cf. Canon 840/2, "Legitime retinetur excessus . . . si pinguis eleemosyna locum pro parte teneat dotis . . . causae piae."

36 Cf. Canon 840/2, "nisi obstet mens fundatoris." Cf. Vermeersch, Epitome, Vol. I, p. 58, n. 108, 5.

CHAPTER XXII

FORFEITED STIPENDS
OR
CANON 841

Having regulated the transfer of stipends, the Code completes its treatment of the subject by elevating these canons to the dignity of laws. It brings this about by attaching to them a sanction which does not constitute a punishment, but which does partake of the nature of a penalty. Since Canon 841 does not constitute a punishment, it has not been put into the fourth book of the Code. Since it does establish some kind of a privation, it is logically placed immediately after the laws which it sanctions.

"Omnes et singuli administratores Causarum piarum aut quoquo modo ad Missarum onera implenda obligati, sive ecclesiastici sive laici, sub exitum cuiuslibet anni, Missarum onera quibus nondum fuerit satisfactum, suis Ordinariis tradant secundum modum ab his definiendum.

"Hoc autem tempus ita est accipiendum ut in Missis ad instar manualium obligatio eas deponendi decurrat a fine illius anni intra quem onera impleri debuissent; in manualibus vero, post annum a die suscepti oneris salva diversa offerentium voluntate." [1]

"Each and every administrator of pious institutions, or any one else who is obliged to attend to the saying of Holy Masses for stipends, whether clerics or laymen, must at the end of each year send to their Ordinaries those stipends for which they have not yet satisfied, according to the manner to be specified by the Ordinary.

"This time is to be understood in such way that for stipends 'ad instar manualium" the obligation of sending them to the Bishop begins with the end of the year dur-

1 Cf. Canon 841.

ing which they should have been said; for manual stipends, one year from the day on which they were received, saving the different will of the givers." [2]

The first section of Canon 841 is taken almost verbatim from the decree "Vigilanti," issued by the Congregation of the Council; [3] whilst the second section of the same canon is based upon the decree "Ut debita," which repeats and interprets the former decree. [4]

The Code's phrase, "administrators of pious institutions" (causarum piarum), has a wider extension than the corresponding phrase in the old law, which divided administrators into beneficiaries and *other* administrators. [5] Hence Blat erroneously restricts the words "pious institutions" to pious foundations. [6] In point of fact the pious institutions referred to in Canon 841 / 1 include not only pious foundations as explained in Canon 1544 / 1, but also religious houses of women under episcopal jurisdiction, parishes and chaplaincies. [7]

Augustine, on the contrary, includes everybody under the term "administrators of pious causes." [8] If this interpretation were correct, then the Code would have

2 Cf. Woywod, "The New Canon Law," p. 169, n. 684.

3 Cf. S. C. C., decr. 25 Maii, 1893, par. "Praeterea"; Cf. A. S. S., Vol. XXVI, p. 58.

4 Cf. S. C. C., decr. 11 Maii, 1904, n. 4; A. S. S., Vol. XXXVI, p. 672. "Cum in decreto 'Vigilanti' diei 25 mensis Maii, 1893, statutum fuerit 'ut in posterum omnes et singuli ubique locorum beneficiati et administratores piarum causarum, aut utcumque ad Missarum onera implenda obligati, sive ecclesiactici sive laici, in fine cuiuslibet anni Missarum onera, quae reliqua sunt, et quibus nondum satisfecerint propriis Ordinariis tradant iuxta modum ab iis definiendum; ad tollendas ambiguitates Emi Patres declarant ac statuunt, tempus his verbis praefinitum ita esse accipiendum, ut pro Missis fundatis aut alicui beneficio adnexis obligatio eas deponendi decurrat a fine illius anni intra quem onera impleri debuissent; pro Missis vero manualibus obligatio eas deponendi incipiat post annum a die suscepti oneris, si agatur de magno Missarum numero; salvis praescriptionibus praecedentis articuli pro minori Missarum numero, aut diversa voluntate offerentium."

5 Cf. S. C. C., decr., "Vigilanti," 25 Maii, 1893; Cf. A. S. S., Vol. XXVI, p. 58.

6 Cf. Blat, Liber III, pars. 1, p. 167, a.

7 Cf. Augustine, "A Commentary," Vol. IV, p. 208.

8 Ibid; Cf. S. C. C., decr. 19 Feb. 1921; Cf. A. A. S., Vol. XIII, p. 230.

inserted a meaningless phrase into Canon 841 / 1 by mentioning those people who are otherwise charged with the celebration of Masses: "aut quoquo modo ad Missarum onera implenda obligati, sive ecclesiastici sive laici." As a matter of fact these latter words refer to individual priests who have superfluous stipends on hand, and especially to negligent or malicious clerics who purposely accumulate these offerings.[9] But these words include also lay executors, heirs, and agents who are obliged to have Masses said for somebody else.[10]

Since the legislator has used the phrase "sub exitum cuiuslibet anni" in preference to its synonym, "in fine cuiuslibet anni," the legal time to send stipends to one's Ordinary is to be reckoned morally, not mathematically, so that a priest need not send *all* his stipends to the Ordinary, but may keep a reasonable supply on hand.[11]

When Canon 841 / 1 refers to "their Ordinaries," it means the Major Superior (*e. g.*, Provincial) of exempt religious; and for non-exempt religious, secular priests and all laymen, it means the Ordinary of the place, *i. e.*, the Bishop, the Vicar General, the administrator of a vacant diocese, Vicar Apostolic, Prefect Apostolic, etc.[12]

The second section of Canon 840 explains the term "year" as used in the first section of the same canon. For founded Masses and quasi-manual Masses, the year is the calendar year; for manual Masses, it is the period of 365 days on which Mass could have been said. For example, a pastor should have applied a founded Mass on October 15, 1924. He could not do so, and therefore transferred it as a quasi-manual Mass to a seminary professor. The professor forgets about the stipend, but remembers it in the afternoon of December 31, 1924. That professor

9 Cf. Blat, Liber III, pars 1, p. 167—b—"cum culpa vel sine ea." Cf. S. C. C., decr. 25 Maii, 1893; Cf. A. S. S., Vol. XXVI, p. 58.

10 Cf. Woywod in The Homiletic and Pastoral Review, 1920-1921, Vol. XXI, p. 922.

11 Cf. Cappello, "De Sacramentis," Vol. I, p. 571, n. 712, ad finem.

12 Cf. Canon 198/1 and Canon 111.

must send the stipend to his Bishop on the very next day, *i. e.*, on January 1, 1925. He may not celebrate the Mass on New Year's Day, for his time has expired at midnight.

A curate, however, who has accepted a manual stipend on July 15, 1924, may keep that intention until July 15, 1925. This statement does not imply that he *should* defer the Mass for a whole year; for Canon 841 does not derogate from Canon 834. This statement means that if a priest has kept an offering for a whole year, he is not allowed to keep it any longer.

As regards the purpose of the law, Canon 841 is intended to check avarice by preventing the accumulation of stipends, to forestall all unreasonable delay on the part of priests, and to protect the faithful departed against a misappropriation of funds on the part of lay executors. [13]

Since Canon 841 is intended to protect the rights of the faithful, not to curtail their privileges, the legislator ends this law with the words, "saving the different will of the givers." [14] This ablative absolute can refer to manual stipends only; for founded Masses, as a rule, have to be celebrated on the day appointed by the founder. [15]

The exception appended to Canon 841 means that if people explicitly or implicitly permit a priest to keep their stipends for more than a year, then he is not obliged to send those offerings to the Bishop at the end of twelve months. Thus, if someone gives a curate money for more Masses than he can be reasonably expected to say within a year, such a person implicitly permits the priest to keep the stipends for more than a year.[16] With all the more reason, may he retain the offerings if the Masses must be said by him personally or in a particular church or at a designated altar; for in this hypothesis,

13 Cf. S. C. C., decr. "Vigilanti," 25 Maii, 1893; Cf. A. S. S., Vol. XXVI, p. 58.

14 Cf. Canon 841/2, "salva diversa offerentium voluntate."

15 Cf. Blat, Liber III, pars. 1, p. 168.

16 Ibid, p. 167; Cf. S. C. C., decr. "Ut debita," 11 Maii, 1904, n. 5.

the donor presumably sacrifices his right of time for the privilege of place or person.[17]

Finally, it may be only a venial sin or even no sin at all to keep without any justifying reason a few stipends for a long time beyond a year, or a large number of stipends for a short time beyond the legal time limit. But, as a rule, this precept of the Chuch imposes on priests a grave obligation (ex genere suo grave) of transferring unsaid Masses to the Bishop at the close of the year.[18]

17 Cf. Cappello, De Sacramentis, Vol. I, p. 571, n. 712, d.
17 Cf. Vermeersch, "Epitome," Vol. II, p. 53, n. 5.
18 Cf. Cappello, l. c., ad finem.

CHAPTER XXIII

Superiors' Vigilance
or
Canon 842

According to Del Giudice, the faithful have no other assurance than the celebrant's own word that they have not been defrauded of their money by a priest who accepted their stipends but failed to say their Masses.[1] The Church refutes this assertion by inserting into her code of laws a canon which obliges Bishops and religious Superiors to see to it that all obligations of Masses are faithfully discharged by their sacerdotal subjects.

For Canon 842 reads as follows: "Ius et officium advigilandi ut onera Missarum adimplentur, in ecclesiis saecularium pertinet ad loci Ordinarium; in religiosorum ecclesiis, ad eorum Superiores."

The right and duty to see that the obligation of the Mass stipends is attended to in secular churches belongs to the Ordinary; in churches of the religious to their Superiors." [2]

In the eighth century, a Council held at Cambray decreed that every priest should give an account of his Masses to the Bishop during Lent. [3] In the diocese of Toledo, a certain Archbishop went even further, demanding that the rectors of churches report to him every three months concerning the stipends received and the Masses celebrated. He even claimed the right of transferring to another church the Mass intentions that were neglected by their original recipients. The case was brought before the Rota on the ground that the Archbishop had exceeded

1 Del Giudice, "Stipendia Missarum," p. 200.

2 Cf. Woywod, "The New Canon Law," p. 169, n. 685.

3 Cf. Berlendi, "Delle Oblazione," p. 208.

his powers; but His Grace was upheld by this august tribunal of the Catholic Church.[4]

Innocent XII instructed the Ordinary to see to it that all founded Masses were celebrated not only in the diocesan churches, but also in monasteries and pious institutes.[5] He extended to all religious Superiors (local or provincial, exempt or non-exempt) the task of superintending the celebration of Masses and of enforcing the laws about stipends. He even threatened these Superiors with removal from office for neglect of this duty.[6]

Two centuries later, the Congregation of the Council obliged the Bishops and other Ordinaries to compel their own priests and to warn the others to comply with the canon law concerning the substitution of books for stipends.[7] On the other hand, the Holy See told a certain Bishop not to inspect the Franciscans' record for manual stipends which they had accepted in a parish church.[8] Finally the Ordinaries were charged with the execution of the decree "Ut debita," the epitome of the old canon law on stipends and the prototype of the present legislation in the Code.[9] Canon 842 shows that the execution of the ecclesiastical laws concerning the manual Masses of exempt or non-exempt religious priests pertains to the local Superior of those clergymen.[10] As regards founded Masses, the term "Superior" is restricted by Canon 1550 to the Major Superior of exempt religious.[11] Since there are no American nuns who are subject to "regular"

4 Cf. Benedict XIV, "De Sacrificio Missae," Appendix VIII, ad lib. III, p. 283.

5 Innocent XII, const. "Nuper," 23 Dec., 1697/8; Cf. Fontes, Vol. I, p. 511.

6 Ibid, No. 24; Fontes, Vol. I, p. 517.

7 Cf. S. C. C., decr. "Vigilanti," 25 Maii, 1893; Cf. A. S. S., Vol. XXVI, p. 58.

8 Cf. S. C. Ep. et Reg., "Sancti Hippolyti, 11 Maii, 1904.

9 Cf. S. C. C., decr. "Ut debita," 11 Maii, 1904, n. 15, ad finem; Cf. A. S. S., Vol. XXXVI, p. 676.

10 Cf. Blat, Liber III, pars. 1, p. 168.

11 Cf. Canon 1550, "Si agatur de piis fundationibus in ecclesiis, etiam paroecialibas, religiosorum exemptorum, iura et officia Ordinarii loci, de quibus in can, 1545-1549, exclusive competunt Superiori maiori."

Superiors, it follows that the Bishop or Vicar General of the diocese has the right and the duty of superintending the celebration of all Masses in the convents of the United States.[12]

This obligation on the part of the Bishop or religious Superior is evidently a serious one.[13] Hence it is but equitable that he be permitted to exercise his vigilance either on the occasion of his canonical visitation or at any other time; and that he may inquire about these matters either in virtue of his office or at the request of some interested person, such as the giver of the stipend or the founder of the Mass.[14]

12 Cf. Augustine, "A Commentary," Vol. IV, p. 210.
13 Cf. Cappello, "De Sacramentis," Vol. I, n. 713, p. 572.
14 Ibid.

CHAPTER XXIV

Parochial Records of Stipends or Canon 843

To facilitate the Superior's vigilance over Mass-obligations; to protect priests against forgetfulness, misunderstanding, scrupulosity; to provide executors with a receipt for a bequest as well as a certificate of the Masses celebrated; and to insure all givers of stipends against the loss of Masses: the Code contains a canon which obliges the rectors of churches and of other pious institutions to keep a Book of Mass Intentions, a book which the Ordinary must inspect at least once a year.[1]

Canon 843 reads as follows: "Rectores ecclesiarum aliorumque piorum locorum sive saecularium sive religiosorum in quibus eleemosynae Missarum recipi solent, peculiarem habeant librum in quo accurate notent Missarum receptarum numerum, intentionem, eleemosynam, celebrationem.

"Ordinarii tenentur obligatione singulis saltem annis huiusmodi libros sive per se sive per alios recognoscendi."

"The rectors of churches and other pious places, both secular and religious, in which stipends for Masses are usually received, must have a special book in which they should accurately mark down the number, intention, amount of stipend, and the celebration of the Masses they receive.

"The Ordinaries are obliged to inspect these books at least once a year, either in person or through some one else."[2]

The Code modeled the present canon on a paragraph

1 Cf. Homiletic and Pastoral Review, Vol. XXI, p. 923.
2 Cf. Woywod, "The New Canon Law," p. 170, n. 686.

in a constitution of Pope Innocent XII.[3] In recent times that old law was modified to the extent of putting the direct burden on the Superiors alone rather than the rectors themselves.[4] The Code goes back to the rigor of the constitution "Nuper," by directly obliging the rectors to record all Masses carefully.

The name of rectors in Canon 843 has a wider range of meaning than it has in Canons 479 and 480. In virtue of Canon 18, the term "rectors," in the present instance, includes pastors, chaplains and all other diocesan or religious priests who have charge of any church or chapel.[5]

An exact pastor will comply with the spirit of the Code by keeping three distinct books for Mass Intentions. In the first book he will record all Masses for which manual or quasi-manual stipends have been received in his church or rectory.

To indicate the *number* of Masses as required by Canon 843, it is sufficient to record the intentions. For the present law does not mean that the priest who receives the stipends from the same person must number those intentions consecutively. The reason why the Code mentions the number of intentions is simply to enable the Bishop to know how many stipends have been received

3 Cf. Innocent XII, const. "Nuper," 23 Dec., 1697/19; Cf. Fontes, Vol. I, p. 516. "Indemque (Rectores, etc.) teneantur pariter in Sacrario duos libros retinere, ac in eorum altero singula onera perpetua, et temporalia, in altero autem Missas Manuales, et tam illorum, quam istarum adimplementum, et elleemosynas distinct, et dilegenter annotare, et annotandas, seu annotanda curare, sigulisque annis de supradictis adimplementis, eleemosynis et oneribus pariter exactam rationem suis Superioribus reddere, ac omnes, et singulas rationes huiusmodi in praefatis respective Libris simili distinctione, et diligentia, tam praefati a quibus rationes debent reddi, quam Superiores, quibus reddendae erunt, describere, seu annotare, sive describendas, vel annotandas respective curare."

4 Cf. S. C. C., decr. "Ut debita, 11 Maii, 1904/15 circa finem; Cf. A. S. S., Vol. XXXVI, p. 676. "Denique officii singulorum Ordinariorum erit curare ut in singulis ecclesiis, praeter tabellam erit curare ut in singulis ecclesiis, paraeter tabellam onerum perpetuorum et librum in quo manuales Missae quae a fidelibus traduntur ex ordine cum sua eleemosyana recenseantrn, insuper habeantur libri in quibus dictorum onerum et Missarum satisfactio signetur."

5 Cf. Blat, Liber III, pars. 1, p. 168, ad finem.

in any particular church and thus to judge whether the rector has accepted too many stipends.

Since a Mass may be celebrated for the unknown intention of the giver, the Mass may be recorded "ad intentionem dantis." [6] Nevertheless, the Christian name of a deceased person should always be mentioned in the book of Mass intentions, so that this name can be inserted into the Oration and the Memento of the Requiem Mass.

The amount of the offering must be indicated in some way. However, only an extraordinary stipend has to be recorded explicitly; for when this is done, then the rest of the offerings are presumed to be the usual diocesan stipend. To show that the obligation has been discharged, a mere check or a line through the intention would fulfil the requirement of Canon 843.

Hence the priest whose book shows nothing but the following entry, "ad int, dant." or at most an occasional line like this: "ad int. dant. 2," could not be accused of violating the precepts of the Code. Nevertheless, it would be far more commendable to buy a regular Book of Mass Intentions, or at least to use an ordinary note-book in which each intention is given a separate line and in which every Mass is recorded as follows:

Date Rec'd	Donor	Amt.	Intention	Date of Celebration	Date Disch'd	Remarks

In addition to the official record of manual Masses, the pastor or chaplain will have another book for founded Masses. [7] This book will be kept in the parish archives; and it will indicate carefully all temporary and perpetual foundations of Masses, the name of the founder, the endowment or capital, the intention, the days on which the Masses are to be said, the dates on which they have been said, reduction if any, the stipend given, etc. [8]

Although it is desirable to have one book for manual

6 Cf. A. K. K., Vol. 68, p. 276, n. 18.

7 Cf. Canon 1549/2. "Pariter praeter librum de quo in can. 843/1, alter liber retineatur et apud rectorem servetur, in quo singula onera perpetua et temporaria eorumque implementum et eleemosynae adnotentur, ut de iis omnibus exacta ratio Ordinario loci reddatur."

8 Cf. Link, Mess-Stipendien, p. 232-2, a.

Masses and another for founded Masses, still two distinct parts of the same book will suffice. A third book which every pastor ought to have is the Announcement Book. The ideal record for this purpose would be a diary in which the pages are so ruled as to assign four or five lines to every day of the year, and in which all the Announced Masses for the week are marked in the space given to the date of their celebration. For example, one entry would look like this:

Tuesday, January 27

6.30—John Doe.
7.00—Richard Roe.
8.00—Nuptial Mass: Wm. Brown and Mary White.
9.00—Solemn Funeral: John Smith.

Wednesday, January 28

6.30—Poor Souls.
7.00—Special Int.
7.30—Blank.
8.00—Month's Mind for Henry Green.

In small parishes and in other places where comparatively few Masses have to be said on specified days, the pastor might be justified in using the ordinary Announcement Book as a diary for his Masses. But in no case should any priest try to use the leaves of his "Ordo," or directory, as a substitute for the official register prescribed by Canon 843 or for the private record recommended in Canon 844.[9]

The reason why the directory should not be substituted for a book of Mass intentions lies in the fact that the second section of Canon 843 obliges the Ordinary to examine at least once a year the official record prescribed in the first section of the same law, whilst Canons 1545-1555 make a similar provision regarding the record of founded Masses.

Vermeersch considers this an obligation on the conscience of the Bishop or Major Superior.[10] The words

9 Cf. Link, Mess-Stipendien, p. 233.

10 Cf. Vermeersch, Epitome Juris Canonici, Vol. II, p. 59.

"singulis annis" imply that this examination must be made more frequently than the canonical visitation. Nay, the adverb "saltem" indicates that the Bishop may inspect the records of his rectors (not of exempt religious priests) as often as he sees fit.[11] Of course, he need not do all this work in person; as the Code plainly states, he may delegate his Vicar General, his vicar forane, or even some other person to examine the books in his stead. Finally, if an obligation of examining the book rests on the Bishop, a fortiori the pastor or chaplain is bound under penalty of mortal sin to keep some kind of a legible record in at least one book of Mass intentions.[12]

11 Cf. Cappello, De Sacramentis, Vol. I, p. 572, n. 714.
12 Ibid, n. 714—2.

CHAPTER XXV

Official and Unofficial Records or Canon 844

The last canon in the title on stipends extends to all Bishops and priests the laws which the preceding canon applies only to the rectors of churches and of other ecclesiastical institutions. The first section of Canon 844 refers to local Ordinaries and religious Superiors in their official capacity; the second section deals with individual priests in their private character.

These are the words of Canon 844: "Ordinarii quoque locorum et superiores religiosi qui propriis subditis aliisve Missas celebrandas committunt, quas acceperint Missas cum suis eleemosynis cito in librum per ordinem referant curentque pro viribus ut quamprimum celebrentur.

"Imo omnes sacerdotes sive saeculares sive religiosi debent accurate adnotare quas quisque Missarum intentiones receperit, quibusve satisfecerit."

"The Ordinaries of dioceses, and religious Superiors, who give Masses to their subjects or to others to say, shall mark down at once the Masses with the alms they receive, in the order in which they get them, and attend to it, that as far as possible they are said soon.

"Every priest, whether secular or religious, must mark down accurately the Mass intentions which they receive, and whether and when they have satisfied them." [1]

Concerning the translation of this canon, it is to be noted that the law is not as strict as Woywod would make it; for the adverb "cito" means "promptly" rather than "at once." [2]

Canon 844 differs in several respects from the old law

1 Cf. Woywod, "The New Canon Law," p. 170, n. 687.

2 Cf. Augustine, "A Commentary," Vol. IV, p. 211.

on which it is based.[3] First the decree "Ut debita" mentioned only the diocesan Ordinaries, *i. e.*, Bishops, administrators, Vicars General, Vicars Apostolic, Prefects Apostolic. The Code adds the term "religious Superiors," which includes not only the General and the provincial, but also any local Superior of an exempt or non-exempt religious community.[4]

Secondly, the Code does not strictly oblige the Bishop or other Superior to supply his own priests with stipends ere he sends such offerings to the Holy See or to foreign priests.[5] Nevertheless, by mentioning "their own subjects" first, the Code insinuates that charity should begin at home and that, ever under the new law, priests of a diocese and the members of a religious community have the first claim upon their Superiors' superfluous stipends.[6]

Then, too, the Code omits the old regulation that ordinarily manual Masses must be said before quasi-manual Masses.[7] Rather the phrase "per ordinem" suggests that, as a rule, Masses ought to be said in the order in which the stipends have been received.[8] Moreover, the adverb "promptly" (cito) relaxes the rigor of the old decree, which used the word "immediately" (statim) to express the time when Bishops must record stipends. Finally, the clause "curentque pro viribus" indicates that the Superiors need not interpret too literally the injunc-

3 Cf. S. C. C., decr. "Ut debita," Maii, 1904, n. 7; Cf. A. S. S., Vol. XXXVI, p. 679. "Ordinarii dioecesani Missas, quas expraecedentium articulorum dispositione coarcevabunt, statim ex ordine in librum cum respectiva eleemosyna referent, et curabunt pro viribus ut quamprimum celebrentur. . ."

4 Cf. Blat, Liber III, pars. 1, p. 169; Cf. S. C. C., decr. 27 Feb. 1905, ad 1; Cf. A. S. S., Vol. XXXVII, p. 526.

5 Cf. S. C. C., decr. "Ut debita," 11 Maii, 1904, n. 7; Cf. A. S. S., Vol. XXXVI, p. 674. "In distributione autem servabunt regulam decreti *'Vigilanti,'* scilicet, Missarum intentiones primum distribuent inter ascerdotes sibi subjectos, qui eis indigere noverint."

6 Ibid; Cf. Blat, Liber III, pars 1, p. 169.

7 Cf. S. C. C., decr. "Ut debita," 11 Maii, 1904, n. 7; "Ita tamen ut prius manualibus satisfiat, deinde iis quae ad instar manualium sunt."

8 Cf. Rugla II, III, XII, in 6°. "Qui prior est tempore potior est iure."

tion to have the Masses celebrated as soon as possible (quamprimum).[9]

Before the Code, there was no general law obliging the individual priest to make a personal record of his Mass intentions.[10] Concerning the book which every priest must now keep, in virtue of Canon 844 / 2, little remains to be said.[11] The object of the law and the consensus of canonists make it certain that he who fails to record three or four of his Masses commits a mortal sin;[12] and if he neglects entirely to keep some kind of a book for this purpose, he may well be accused of a permanent crime.[13]

In fine, though the Code contains twenty canons on manual stipends alone and several other laws[14] which refer in some way to these offerings, there still remain obligations of charity which the conscientious priest will not ignore. Should he receive but a trifle, the true shepherd of his flock will, if possible, announce the Mass, or at least inform the giver when it will be said.[15] If the rubrics permit, the devout priest will celebrate the votive Mass which conforms to the intention of the postulant. Though his purse be swelled with the gold of the rich, the ambassador of Christ will accept the widow's mite, and will graciously offer to find another priest to say the Mass at her request.[16] The servant of the servants of God will not brand himself with the stigma of a Simon Magus; nor will he sell his Master for a piece of silver.[17]

9 Cf. Bargilliat, "Les Honoraires De Messes," p. 40.

10 Cf. Blat, Liber III, pars. 1, p. 170.

11 Cf. Chapter XXIV of this book.

12 Cf. Cappello, De Sacramentis, Vol. I, p. 573, n. 714-5; Blat, Liber III, pars. 1, p. 170; Vermeersch, Epitome, Vol. II, p. 59, n. 109.

13 Cf. Canones 2222/1; 2195; 841/1; 2324. Cf. Sole, "De Delictis et poenis," p. 249. A permanent crime (delictum successivum) consists of one act (e. g., apostasy, abduction) as opposed to a habitual crime consisting of repeated acts (blasphemy).

14 Cf. Canons 806, 809, 918/2, 2408, 1509, n. 5; 466/3, 339, 1515, 1544-1551, 727, 730, 2222, 2237, 2324, 1303/2, 1506, 1517, 2321.

15 Cf. Link, "Mess-Stipendien," p. 217, n. 7.

16 Cf. Link, "Mess-Stipendien," p. 217, n. 7.

17 Cf. p. 17, "Turpius Christum vendimus quam Judas."

Yet, when the occasion presents itself, the zealous pastor will not hesitate to inform his flock about the real nature of Mass stipends. At some Holy Hour, perchance, the zealous priest will tell his hearers the story of the poor woman's prayer that outbalanced all the meat that the butcher could give; and then he will point out the fact that a dollar can never balance the infinite worth of the Eucharistic Sacrifice. After that, the well-informed preacher will trace for his audience the gradual development of the modern stipend from the ancient oblations. Next he will carefully explain how the giver of a stipend takes an active part in the unbloody offering of Calvary's Victim.[18] Thus will the priest of God teach the faithful to look upon a Mass stipend as the layman's acceptable sacrifice and the celebrant's irreprehensible remuneration.[19]

18 Cf. Tanquerey, "Synopsis Theol. Dogmaticae," Vol. III, n. 711, p. 497, New York, 1920, Ed. 17. "Fideles dicuntur offerre sacrificium Missae non quidem immediate et proprie loquendo, sed mediate et improprie . . . sive ministrando altari, siv materiam sacrificii praebendo, aut stipendium erogando."

19 Cf. Linzer Quartalschrift, 1924, IV Heft, p. 747-753.

VITA

Charles Frederick Keller, the son of Joseph and Mary Keller, was born in Mahanoy City, Pa., on December 30, 1898, and he was baptized in St. Fidelis' Church on January 1, 1899. Having studied for six years in the parochial school and for four years in the public schools of his native town, he was admitted at the age of sixteen to the second year of the classical department in the diocesan seminary at Overbrook, Pa. Eight years later, on May 26, 1923, he was ordained to the priesthood in the Cathedral of S S. Peter and Paul by His Eminence, Dennis J. Dougherty, Cardinal Archbishop of Philadelphia.

On October 2nd of the same year, Rev. Charles Keller matriculated as one of the first post-graduate students in the newly founded School of Canon Law at the Catholic University, Washington, D. C. In the same month, he qualified for the degree of Bachelor of Sacred Theology (S. T. B.); and a month later, for the Baccalaureate of Canon Law (J. C. B.). During his first year at the University, Father Keller pursued courses in public, international, and canon law. At the end of the term, on June 11, 1924, he received the degree of Licentiate in Canon Law (J. C. L.), the subject of his dissertation being Canon 824 / 1. During his second year in Washington, Roman law was added to his other branches of civil and canon law. To obtain the degree of Doctor in Canon Law (J. C. D.), he wrote and published the present dissertation on Mass Stipends.

DEUS LUX MEA

CANONES

QUOS

AD DOCTORATUS GRADUM

IN

IURE CANONICO

APUD UNIVERSITATEM CATHOLICAM AMERICAE
CONSEQUENDUM
PUBLICE PROPUGNABIT

CAROLUS FREDERICUS KELLER

SACERDOS ARCHIDIOECESIS PHILADELPHIENSIS
IURIS CANONICI LICENTIATUS

Hora III P. M. Die XVIII Maii A. D. MCMXXV

Universitas Catholica Americae
Washingtonii, D. C.
Sacra Facultas Canonica
1924-1925

No. 27

THESES

I. De forma regiminis in Ecclesia.
II. De potestate temporali Romani Pontificis.
III. De iure instituendi alumnos clericales.
IV. De iure instituendi scholas.
V. De iure censurandi libros.
VI. De iure civili quoad matrimonia.
VII. Canones 1-6. De Codicis ambitu.
VIII. " 8-11. De legibus ecclesiasticis.
IX. " 12-14. De legum subiectis.
X. " 15-16. De legum effectibus.
XI. " 17-24. De legum interpretatione.
XII. " 82-86. De dispensationibus.
XIII. " 118-123. De iuribus et privilegiis clericorum.
XIV. " 519-523. De speciali religiosae confessario.
XV. " 727-730. De simonia.
XVI. Canon 824. De Missarum stipendiis in genere.
XVII. Canones 828-831. De obligatione celebrandi Missam ratione stipendii.
XVIII. " 834-836. De tempore celebrandi Missam ratione stipendii.
XIX. Canon 840. De transmissione stipendii integri.
XX. " 1917. De sponsalibus.
XXI. Canones 1043-1046. De casibus Matrimonii urgentioribus.
XXII. " 1250-1254. De abstinentia et ieiunio.
XXIII. " 1327-1328. De divini verbi praedicatione.
XXIV. Canon 1367. De officiis seminaristarum.
XXV. " 1455. De privilegiis patronorum.
XXVI. Canones 1556-1558. De incompetentia absoluta.

XXVII. Canon 1560. De foro necessario.
XXVIII. Canones 1561-1568. De competentia iudicis.
XXIX. " 1606-1607. De tribunali delegato.
XXX. " 1679-1683. De actione ob nullitatem actorum.
XXXI. " 1706-1710. De libello.
XXXII. " 1892-1897. De querela nullitatis.
XXXIII. " 2195-2198. De notione delicti.
XXXIV. " 2215-2219. De notione poenarum.
XXXV. " 2241-2244. De censuris in genere.
XXXVI. Canon 2367. De absolutione complicis.
XXXVII. " 2368. De crimine solicitationis.
XXXVIII. " 2369. De violatione sigilli.
XXXIX. Slavery.
XL. Manumission.
XLI. Citizenship.
XLII. Patria Potestas.
XLIII. Non-catholics in Roman law.
XLIV. Guardianship.
XLV. Guarantees of guardianship.
XLVI. Corporations.
XLVII. Foundations.
XLVIII. Sponsalia.
XLIX. Conception and form of Roman marriage.
L. Modifications of personality.
LI. The nature of international law.
LII. The sources of international law.
LIII. The immunity of diplomatic agents.
LIV. Extradition.
LV. The Monroe Doctrine.
LVI. A State's right of self-defense.
LVII. Methods falling short of war.
LVIII. Belligerency.
LIX. Person of enemies.
LX. Vessels.

INDEX

www.ingramcontent.com/pod-product-compliance
Lightning Source LLC
LaVergne TN
LVHW050225080826
844660LV00012B/472
* 9 7 8 0 8 1 3 2 2 2 1 7 2 *